QUICK COOKING *for* BUSY PEOPLE

— families — first-time cooks — singles —

Dedication

For my children and their families,
who made it necessary for me to be a quick cook,
and who each day meet the challenges of eating well
and living joyfully.

Karen

D1445561

Pictured on Cover
Chicken Curry, page 115

Quick Cooking for Busy People
by
Karen Wokes

First Printing – January 2000

Copyright © 2000 by
Sandy Hook Publishing
Box 202
Sandy Hook, Manitoba, Canada R0C 2W0
Telephone: (204) 389-2005

Canadian Cataloguing in Publication Data

Wokes, Karen

Quick cooking for busy people

Includes index.
ISBN 1-894022-42-4

1. Quick and easy cookery.   I. Title

TX833.5.W64 2000   641.5'55   C00-920004-5

Photography by: Patricia Holdsworth
Patricia Holdsworth Photography, Regina, Saskatchewan

Dishes, Accessories and Flowers courtesy of:
Sandstone Gift Essentials
Gimili, Manitoba R0C 1B0
204-642-9020 FAX: 204-642-9030

Page Formatting and Index by Iona Glabus

Designed, Printed and Produced in Canada by:
Centax Books, a Division of Publishing Solutions/PW Group
Publishing Director, Photo Designer & Food Stylist: Margo Embury
1150 Eighth Avenue, Regina, Saskatchewan, Canada S4R 1C9
(306) 525-2304   FAX (306) 757-2439
E-mail: centax@printwest.com   www.centaxbooks.com

TABLE OF CONTENTS

 Super-Quick Logo – This logo identifies super-quick recipes throughout the book. These are recipes that take 10-15 minutes to prepare.

Recipes have been tested in U.S. Standard measurements. Common metric measurements are given as a convenience for those who are more familiar with metric. Recipes have not been tested in metric.

INTRODUCTION

I like to cook and I enjoy the pleasure and appreciation of my family and friends as we share a meal. BUT . . . I don't like to cook every day. Put simply, it can be tedious and difficult though, for all of us, necessary. **I have designed this book to meet the challenge of preparing good healthy meals in less time than it takes to have a pizza delivered.**

Over the years, I have found that the majority of cookbooks are chock-full of wonderful food combinations and flavors as well as beautiful, glossy photos. But they are designed to sell, and to feed our fantasies as well as our bodies. They are not very practical when the 6:15 deadline for dinner looms. When cooking for family and friends, I found that I could prepare a satisfying meal in a very short time and be pleased with the results. This book is a collection of recipes and time and energy-saving tips that have helped me bring dinner to the table at 6:15 p.m. every day.

As busy people we need meal ideas that are ready in minutes. These recipes can be prepared in less than 30 minutes and use ingredients usually kept on hand or purchased on the weekly "big shop". This book also includes tips for planning and shopping and a list of pots, pans and other tools needed.

There are recipes for everyday favorites, for quick meals and snacks and recipes for when you have that desperate feeling and just can't face the kitchen – AGAIN. These recipes are designed to be low in fat and cholesterol. The choice of butter, oil or margarine and the amount of salt used is up to you. Many recipes have variations and suggest accompaniments. Preparation is dependent on the use of a few basic pieces of kitchen equipment. Good quality, heavy non-stick pans, a pasta or stock pot and good steel knives – sharp – are the keys.

Research tells us that as cooks we have 3 to 4 recipes in our head that become standbys for daily meal preparation, and that most cooks plan dinner at 5:00 p.m.

It is my hope that this book will expand the number of recipes stored in your head, help in planning and preparation and, most importantly, be a ready, well-used reference for quick and healthy meals every day.

PLANNING AND SHOPPING

I have prepared meals for 7 people every day for more years than I wish to state. I never felt that I had the time or interest in filling in a day-to-day weekly meal planner, but I have developed a method that works for me. Perhaps it will also work for you.

As a hurried cook, I find it is helpful to:

- Think and plan ahead. I do that before I shop and with flyers at hand.

- Keep a well-stocked pantry.

- Keep a master list of ingredients for basic cooking to help remind me of what is needed.

- Keep a needs list on the fridge and add the items that I run out of or need, and encourage others in the household to do the same.

- Do my big shop once a week and try to shop at a non-peak time, such as early morning, early afternoon or late evening.

- I welcome help in the meal preparation and cleanup and I am willing to ask family members for help and give directions.

Planning:

- I plan ahead and think of the week as 7 meal choices – Sunday to Saturday.

- With the weekly flyer of my favorite supermarket in hand, and foods that we like to eat in mind, I start with the meat/protein needs of the main meal for each day. For example, chicken thighs are on sale, I buy double so that I have a second meal. Two meals taken care of.

- That leaves 5 choices to make. Italian sausage, pork loin, ground meat, beef and eggs are my choices. I keep in mind quantities needed, taste preferences and the amount of time that I have to cook.

- I list the meat or egg choices on the left hand side of a piece of paper and think of a dish that they will become. These are the main meal choices for the week. A well-stocked pantry ensures the other meals can sort of take care of themselves.

Shopping:

- With the weekly plan on paper, I add a column of ingredients needed for the main meal choices.

- I do a visual check of the pantry and fridge and add those needs to the list.

- I add the weekly needs list from the fridge.

- I think lunches, breakfasts and snacks and add those needs.

- Finally, I add household items such as soaps and paper products.

- To facilitate shopping, I make sure my final list is divided roughly into store departments.

Planning and shopping for 21 meals, plus snacks, and being prepared for the unexpected is a big job and hard work. Don't undervalue this task.

Planning helps and makes life easier, but plans change. There is always room for variations or a missed meal or the inclusion of an impromptu picnic or treat.

EQUIPMENT AND TOOLS

As a quick cook, you will not be happy in the kitchen unless you have the tools you need. Here is a list of essentials and desirables for meal preparation.

You will need:

- **2 non-stick skillets or pans**, a large and medium size, with lids. Good-quality heavy-based pans make cooking quicker, safer and more enjoyable, and they are easy to clean.
- Small and large saucepans with lids.
- A **Dutch oven** or heavy-bottomed pot.
- A **pasta pot** with a **strainer** or a **stock pot** with a **colander** for draining pasta.
- **4 knives**: an **8" (20 cm) blade** for chicken, fish, meat and vegetables and general use. I find I can carve most things with it as well; a **10" (25 cm) chef's knife** for chopping and slicing, cutting up chicken and vegetables; a **3-4" (8-10 cm) blade paring knife** for vegetables and fruit; and a **serrated bread knife** for breads and some fruits and vegetables. Buy high-carbon stainless steel blades. They are pricy but they're a lifetime investment and they help to make food preparation a pleasure. Buy a **knife sharpener**, the kind with the little steel and ceramic sharpening wheels that you draw or roll the blade over. Wash the blades and wipe them clean. Store your knives in a special place, like a drawer or a wall-mounted holder. It is good to have them sharpened professionally every year or two. Do not put them in the dishwasher; it dulls the edges.
- **Spoons**, **spatulas**, **tongs** and **wooden utensils** for your non-stick pans.
- **Kitchen scissors** and a **vegetable parer** that works, the comfort-grip kinds are excellent.
- A **can opener**, the good-quality cushioned-handled type.
- **2-cup (500 mL) glass measuring cups** (useful for quick-cooking vegetables in the microwave as well as for mixing and measuring).
- Sets of **measuring cups and spoons**.

EQUIPMENT
AND TOOLS *continued*

- **Chopping boards** – medium-sized and small ones for little jobs (you can put them in the dishwasher).
- **Food graters**, **a garlic press** and an assortment of **spoons and spatulas.**
- **Electric hand mixer**.
- **Food processor** – an electric one if you like. There is a good manual one in the housewares department for under $20.00.
- **Rice Cooker/Vegetable Steamer** (optional).
- **Microwave** and **toaster ovens**.
- **2 cookie sheets** and a **pizza pan**.
- A **9 x 13 x 2½" (23 x 33 x 6 cm) pan**, and an **8 x 8 x 2½" (20 x 20 x 6 cm) pan**
- glass and aluminum **pie plates**.
- **oven/microwave-safe covered dishes** or **casseroles**, look for the dishes where the lid becomes a pie plate or shallow dish.
- **Mixing bowls** and **food storage bowls** and **containers**.
- **Microwave dish toppers** – more convenient and they save on plastic wrap.
- **Parchment paper** to line cookie sheets and pizza pans – saves on cleanup time.

F O O D
S A F E T Y

For a period of time our family lived in West Africa. With four children, one a baby, my primary concern was to make sure that the food we were eating was carefully prepared, cooked and stored. One day our cook raised his hands in despair and said "Wash um, wash, um, wash um! All the time, wash um." That was and is the major key to safe food preparation. Wash it!

- Keep the kitchen clean with hot soap and water.
- **Wash your hands often and make sure others working with food do so also.**
- When you are working quickly and preparing a multi-step meal, keep a bowl of warm soapy water close by for quick hand rinsing.
- Wash cutting boards and knives frequently with soap and hot water. Rinse well. Store the boards upright on the counter to dry.
- Change your kitchen cloths and sponges daily. Wash them and your kitchen towels often.
- Keep the counters clean.
- Never eat raw chicken, meat or fish.
- For safe chicken, meat and fish handling, refrigerate as soon as possible after purchase. When ready to use, open the packages over the sink. Dispose of the wrappings in the garbage immediately and place the meat, chicken or fish on a clean plate, or process or cook immediately. If the meat, etc. or wrappings have come in contact with the sink, wash and rinse it right away.
- Wash, rinse and dry all produce, even "prewashed".
- Cover and refrigerate leftovers immediately after each meal. Food cools more quickly on the open wire shelves of the refrigerator than on the solid bottom one.

Food safety measures are critical. They take only moments and may save a life or prevent serious illness.

TIME-SAVING IDEAS

These are some of the things I do to prepare good meals quickly:

- Keep the kitchen reasonably tidy with clear counters and dishes done.
- Have the right equipment and tools to do the job.
- Organize the space in the kitchen so that tools and ingredients are handy to where they are used.
- Have a store of recipes in mind and a ready reference (favorite cookbooks and a clippings file) for more.
- Keep a well-stocked pantry and fridge and a method to keep it that way, which means make time to plan meals and shop.
- Rely on some basic convenience foods such as washed-and-ready-to-eat salads, prepared meats and vegetables, canned beans, tomato products, tuna and salmon.
- When preparing a meal, double the amount and freeze for a second meal or cook extra meat or sauce for a second meal. Sometimes I make soup, prepare meat or chicken, or bake a batch of cookies for dessert or lunch while I am tidying the kitchen.
- Cook large amounts of often-used ingredients, like ground meat, chicken and rice; divide into convenient amounts; label and freeze.
- Ask for help and assign tasks.

In the cooking area:

- Keep oils, vinegars, herbs, spices and other flavoring agents in a cabinet near the stove or on the counter at the right side for you.
- Replace old spices, herbs and condiments from time to time. They lose their lovely fresh impact.
- Keep the tools needed for stove-top cooking at hand, near the stove.

In the pantry:

- Keep like foods together and the ones used most often, such as all the tomato and bean varieties, in one spot up front. I have a spot for broths and soups, and for fruits and miscellaneous. Next, a space for rice and pasta products and a spot for ethnic foods.
- Plastic baskets help to keep small things in order.

In the fridge:

The fridge door works best for all the small jars and bottles, with the least-used items in the bottom row. The most-accessed items, like milk and juice, are on the top shelf. I find the key to the best use of the fridge, and easy rotation and replacement, is keeping things in the same place. Then I can see at a glance where things are and what I need. Yes, I know it is almost impossible to maintain.

For an accessible fridge, it helps to eat rather than store the leftovers, to buy fewer condiments and get rid of the time-expired and rarely-used ones. I keep cheese packages in a small plastic basket so that I can find them when I need them.

In the freezer:

The freezer is my biggest asset and my biggest frustration. Like most people, I am not sure what is on the bottom in the left-hand corner. If you have a similar problem, try this idea: use large freezer-weight ziplock bags to store frozen food and meals in your fridge freezer and chest freezer. Label the bags meat, vegetables, cheese, nuts, etc. I have a bag for cooked rice portions and a bag for bread, such as 2 bagels and half a baguette. It really helps, and because the bags keep the smaller items and containers in order, and the bags stack fairly well, it prevents the tumble-down crash effect that happens so often when you open the door of the fridge freezer or move something in the chest freezer.

S T A R T E R S

Dips, spreads, tortilla, pita, bagel and baguette crisps, bruschetta, wraps

These quickly prepared starters are designed to ease the pangs of hunger. They are prepared from what is on hand and are nutritious too. Try the quesadillas and bruschetta for lunch or with soup or salad.

QUICK STARTERS

These amounts give a taste to 4 people. Double amounts for more snackers.

Creamy Veggie Dips

to:

¾ cup	yogurt	175 mL
¼ cup	mayonnaise	60 mL

add:

4 oz.	can rinsed, drained, broken shrimp	113 g
½ tsp.	curry powder	2 mL
¼ tsp.	salt	1 mL

OR:

½ tsp.	dried dill OR basil	2 mL
1 tsp.	lemon juice	5 mL
	salt and pepper	

OR:

1	green onion, chopped	1
1	garlic clove, minced	2

OR:

1 cup	minced cucumber,	250 mL
½ tsp.	dried dillweed	2 mL

OR:

¼ cup	hot or medium salsa	60 mL
2	green onions, finely chopped	2

Serve with assorted raw vegetables and/or crackers and breads.

Cream Cheese Spreads

Combine:

8 oz.	cream cheese, softened	250 g
2 tbsp.	yogurt OR mayonnaise	30 mL

add:

4 oz.	can rinsed, drained, broken shrimp	113 g
½ tsp.	EACH curry powder, salt	2 mL

OR:

2 oz.	smoked salmon, chopped	55 g
½ tsp.	dried dillweed	2 mL
1 tsp.	lemon juice	5 mL

Combine:

4 oz.	cream cheese	125 g
2 tbsp.	mayonnaise	30 mL
1 tsp.	lemon juice	5 mL

add:

1 tsp.	prepared horseradish	5 mL
2 oz.	smoked salmon, chopped	55 g

OR:

2 ozs.	garlic OR herb feta cheese, crumbled	55 g

Place:

4 or 8 oz.	cream cheese	125 or 250 g
	on a serving plate	
	cover with hot pepper jelly or mango chutney	

Serve with assorted crackers or breads.

Tortilla, Pita, Bagel and Baguette Crisps

Toasting specialty breads means you are never out of crackers. The other advantages are that they are low in fat and can be made from those less-than-fresh leftovers and that end piece of baguette.

Tortilla Crisps

- Brush tortillas lightly on both sides with cooking or olive oil. Cut into wedges with scissors, pizza cutter or knife. Place on a cookie sheet. Sprinkle with a little salt or herbs if you like. Heat at 375°F (180°C) until crisp, about 5 minutes.

Pita Crisps

- Split pitas and process as above.

Bagels

- Cut bagels in half vertically, then into very thin slices horizontally. On a cookie sheet, bake at 300°F (150°C) until dry and crisp, 15-20 minutes. Use as crackers for dips and spreads.

Baguettes – as crackers or canape bases

- Cut day-old bread into very thin slices. On a cookie sheet, bake at 300°F (150°C) for 15-20 minutes.

TIP: When you need only 2 or 3 servings, use the toaster oven.

Santa Fe Cheddar Spread

1 cup	grated Cheddar cheese	250 mL
¼ cup	sour cream	60 mL
¼ cup	salsa	60 mL
2	garlic cloves, minced	2

Combine all the ingredients in a small bowl. Serve with crackers and crisps.

Makes 1¼ cups (300 mL)

Ham and Spinach Pinwheels

Quick to make and good for you too.

10 oz.	bag fresh spinach leaves	283 g
8 oz.	cream cheese	250 g
2 tbsp.	mayonnaise	30 mL
1 tbsp.	creamy mustard spread	15 mL
3	8" (20 cm) flour tortillas	3
6 slices	good quality ham	6 slices

- Wash and stem only as much spinach as needed.

- Mix cream cheese and mayonnaise to soften. Add mustard and mix. Spread on tortillas.

- Cover cheese with spinach leaves. Add a layer of ham slices.

- Roll up tortillas neatly and firmly. Wrap in plastic wrap and let set in fridge for an hour, or overnight if you wish to prepare ahead.

- Cut in 1" (2.5 cm) slices and serve on a plate garnished with lettuce leaves.

Makes about 20 pinwheels

Variation: Try any of your favorite sandwich combos. For **Smoked Salmon Pinwheels** use a cream cheese/mayonnaise mixture and add 1 tbsp. (15 mL) of horseradish, a sprinkle of dried or fresh dillweed and slices of smoked salmon.

TIP: For a neater looking pinwheel, trim the rounded edge off each side of the tortilla before you roll it.

For quick salads and sandwiches, especially in the summer, keep canned salmon, tuna, crushed pineapple and olives in the fridge. It is also wise to have a couple of varieties of beans, chickpeas and hard-boiled eggs to add to salad greens and as the basis for mixed salads and slaws.

Mushroom Basil Bruschetta

1 lb.	mushrooms (wild, button or shiitake), chopped	500 g
1	onion, finely chopped	1
2	garlic cloves, crushed or 1 tsp. (5 mL) bottled, chopped garlic	2
1 tbsp.	olive oil	15 mL
	salt and freshly ground pepper	
1/4 cup	chopped fresh basil or 1 tsp. (5 mL) dried	60 mL
1	baguette	1
1/4 cup	freshly grated Parmesan	60 mL

- Combine mushrooms, onions, garlic and oil in a non-stick pan over medium heat. Cook and stir until soft, about 7 minutes. Add salt, pepper and basil. Cook and stir until well mixed.

- Meanwhile, cut bread into 1" (2.5 cm) slices. Spread on a cookie sheet. Broil each side until lightly toasted.

- Brush bread slices lightly with olive oil.

- Spread mushroom mixture on bread slices. Sprinkle with Parmesan cheese.

- Broil until heated and golden. Serve immediately.

Serves 12

Variation: For **Tomato Basil Bruschetta,** in place of mushroom mixture, combine 1 cup (250 mL) chopped tomato, 1/4 cup (60 mL) chopped fresh basil or 1 tsp. (5 mL) dried, 1 garlic clove, crushed, salt and pepper. Mix and let stand 15 minutes. Toast bread and top with tomato mixture and freshly grated Parmesan. Grill as above.

TIP: Leftover mushroom or tomato mixtures may be added to any soup, pasta or meat dish.

SOUPS AND BREADS

LUNCHES &
LIGHT MEALS

Soups, sandwiches and snacks, potatoes and toppings

Ginger Pumpkin Soup

A savory, colorful soup for fall, it is ready to eat in 10 minutes.

2 cups	pumpkin purée (canned or fresh)	500 mL
1½ cups	chicken or vegetable stock (if using canned broth, buy low salt variety)	375 mL
1 cup	orange juice	250 mL
½ tsp.	onion powder	2 mL
1 tsp.	ground ginger	5 mL
½ tsp.	salt	2 mL
14 oz.	can 2% evaporated milk OR 2 cups (500 mL) whole milk OR 10% cream	398 mL
	pepper to taste	
	yogurt or sour cream as garnish	

*H*ere are some good things to eat at lunch or when you come home late and just can't face the thought of preparing a meal. All the recipes presented here are healthful, flavorful and fast.

- In a large saucepan, combine pumpkin, broth, orange juice, onion powder, ginger and salt.

- Heat over medium-high heat. Stir; bring to a boil; reduce heat and simmer, covered, for 5 minutes. Add milk and heat gently; do not boil. Add pepper and garnish with a little yogurt or sour cream.

Serves 4

Variation: Add ½ lb. (250 g) of diced ham.

Pictured on page 17.

California Medley Soup

We had this soup in a small restaurant in Fargo, North Dakota. It is delicious. Serve with large slices of French bread.

2 tbsp.	butter	30 mL
2 tbsp.	chicken broth OR water	30 mL
1	medium onion, chopped	1
1/3 cup	flour	75 mL
10 oz.	can chicken broth or 1 1/4 cups (300 mL) reconstituted chicken broth	284 mL
2 cups	water	500 mL
1 1/4 cups	10% cream, milk OR 10 oz. (300 mL) can of 2% evaporated milk	300 mL
8 oz.	medium or old Cheddar cheese, grated	250 g
1 tsp.	dry mustard	5 mL
	salt and pepper to taste	
1 lb.	pkg. international mix – California medley, frozen vegetables*	500 g

- Heat a large saucepan over medium-high heat. Add butter, broth and onions. Stir until onions are soft, about 3 minutes. Reduce heat a bit.

- Stir in flour until absorbed.

- Gradually add chicken broth and water, stirring constantly. Add milk. Bring soup almost to a boil. Cook and stir 3-4 minutes.

- Add cheese. Reduce heat to low. Stir to blend. Add mustard, salt and pepper. (Do not boil. If the soup is too hot, the cheese will break down and the soup will appear curdled.)

- Meanwhile, or before you begin, cook frozen vegetables in the microwave as directed on the package. Cut the larger pieces in half. Add to the soup; heat and serve.

Serves 6-8

* If you have fresh vegetables on hand and have time, use 4 cups (1 L) chopped broccoli, cauliflower, asparagus, etc., as you wish. Precook the vegetables in the MICROWAVE for 10 minutes.

Variation: Add 1 cup (250 mL) of chopped ham.

TIPS: If the soup is too thick, add more milk or broth. For a creamy soup with beautiful color and loads of food value use 2% evaporated milk; 10% cream makes a rich creamy soup or choose milk.

Pictured on page 17.

Minestrone

The ham in this soup is optional, omit it if you choose. I like the additional flavor that it adds.

1 tsp.	vegetable oil	5 mL
1/4 lb.	deli country ham, chopped in small cubes	125 g
1	medium onion, chopped	1
2 tsp.	bottled, minced garlic	10 mL
3 cups	frozen vegetables OR a combo of what you have on hand – carrot, celery, cabbage, green peppers, and/or chopped spinach	750 mL
1 tbsp.	dried basil	15 mL
28 oz.	can diced tomatoes	796 mL
8 cups	broth or 8 cups (2 L) water with 3 tsp. (15 mL) beef bouillon granules	2 L
1 cup	small pasta such as orzo or elbow macaroni	250 mL
1 tsp.	salt	5 mL
1/2 tsp.	ground pepper	2 mL

- Heat the oil in a large soup pot over medium-high heat. Add the ham and cook 2-3 minutes. Add the onion and garlic; stir and cook for 2 minutes.

- Add the vegetables, basil, tomatoes, water or broth. Increase heat; stir and cook until the soup is boiling.

- Add the pasta, salt and pepper and bring to a boil. Reduce heat and simmer for 10 minutes. If the soup is too thick add more broth or water. Freeze in family-sized batches.

Makes 10-12 cups (2-3 L)

Variation: When you add 2 x 14 oz. (398 mL) cans of white or kidney beans, rinsed and drained, this recipe makes a delicious soup/stew.

Variations: In place of ham, use 1/2 lb. (250 g) cooked, drained ground beef, pork or turkey. The addition of **chili-style** red kidney beans makes a southwest version – a new taste to enjoy.

TIP: To have the Minestrone and Beef and Tortellini soups cooked and ready in 30 minutes takes some pretty fast chopping and stirring. The extra time invested means soup for dinner and extra meals in the freezer. These soups are my favorites for Friday suppers or Saturday lunches.

Beef and Tortellini Soup

On a cold night or a blustery day, serve this meal-in-a-pot.

2 tbsp.	butter OR margarine	30 mL
½ lb.	top sirloin, cut into ½" (1.3 cm) pieces	250 g
2 tbsp.	flour	30 mL
1	medium onion, chopped	1
2	celery stalks, chopped	2
1	large carrot, chopped	1
1 tsp.	bottled, minced garlic	5 mL
½ tsp.	dried powdered thyme	2 mL
½ tsp.	EACH salt and pepper	2 mL
2 x 10 oz.	cans beef broth	2 x 284 mL
3 cups	water	750 mL
28 oz.	can diced tomatoes and juice OR whole tomatoes, chopped	796 mL
9 oz.	pkg. beef tortellini	280 g
2 tbsp.	flour	30 mL
1 tbsp.	cornstarch	15 mL
½ cup	water	125 mL

- Heat butter in a large pot or Dutch oven over medium-high heat.

- Toss meat in flour and add to pan. Cook until meat is lightly browned. Transfer to a bowl.

- Add onion, celery, carrot and garlic to pan. You may need to add a little oil. Stir and cook until lightly browned, about 3 minutes. Stir in thyme, salt and pepper.

- Add broth, water, tomatoes, reserved beef and tortellini. Bring to a boil; reduce heat and simmer until tortellini are cooked, 10-15 minutes.

- To thicken, mix flour, cornstarch and water in a cup until smooth. Stir into the soup. Bring to a boil and boil 1 minute.

Makes 10-12 cups (2.5-3 L)

Variation: Add chopped green pepper and 1 cup (250 mL) frozen corn niblets when you add the cooked beef and tortellini.

Variation: For a vegetarian version use cheese-filled pasta and replace the sirloin with a can of kidney beans.

TIP: Refrigerate soup for up to 3 days; or freeze leftovers for another meal.

Pictured on page 17.

Lentil and Pasta Soup

Here is a quick version of a nourishing soup. It is a meal in a bowl.

1 tsp.	vegetable oil	5 mL
1	medium onion, chopped	1
2	celery stalks, chopped	2
3 cups	water OR broth	750 mL
12 oz.	can vegetable juice cocktail (such as V8)	341 mL
1 cup	frozen mixed vegetables	250 mL
1 tsp.	bottled minced garlic	5 mL
1/2 cup	small pasta	125 mL
19 oz.	can lentils, drained	540 mL
1 tsp.	EACH parsley flakes and dried oregano	5 mL
1 tsp.	salt	5 mL
1/2 tsp.	pepper	2 mL

- In a Dutch oven or soup pot, heat oil over medium-high heat. Add onion and celery and cook until soft, 3-5 minutes.

- Add water, juice, vegetables, garlic, pasta and lentils. Heat and stir. Bring to a boil and add parsley, oregano, salt and pepper. Reduce heat and simmer about 10 minutes.

Makes 9 cups (2.25 L)

Leftover stew, chicken or chili dishes may be added to soups. Add stews and chili to minestrone, and add leftover chicken dishes to the Lentil and Pasta Soup.

Red and Black Bean Soup

This quickly prepared, everything-in-the-pot-at-once soup is a meal in a bowl.
Serve with chunks of crusty bread and cheese or hot biscuits.

28 oz.	can diced tomatoes	796 mL
3 cups	water, broth OR vegetable juice	750 mL
5½ oz.	can tomato paste	156 mL
1 tbsp.	chili powder	15 mL
1 tsp.	ground cumin	5 mL
1 tsp.	dried basil	5 mL
1 tsp.	salt	5 mL
½ tsp.	pepper	2 mL
19 oz.	can black beans, drained	540 mL
19 oz.	can kidney beans, drained	540 mL
1 tsp.	bottled minced garlic	5 mL
1 cup	finely chopped carrots	250 mL
1 cup	finely chopped celery	250 mL
1	medium onion, chopped	1
14 oz.	can kernel corn	398 mL

- In a Dutch oven or soup pot, combine the first 10 ingredients, up to and including the beans. Heat on high until boiling. Reduce heat and simmer about 10 minutes.

- Meanwhile, chop vegetables and add to soup. Bring soup to a boil; reduce heat and simmer until the vegetables are cooked, about 10 minutes.

Makes 10-12 cups (2.5-3 L)

TIP: Add the vegetables that you have on hand or the ones you prefer. Try zucchini, green beans, chopped spinach or potato.

P I Z Z A

Quick Pizzas

Spread prebaked pizza dough or flatbread with 1/2 cup (125 mL) tomato sauce. Sprinkle with 1/2 cup (125 mL) of shredded Mozzarella or pizza combo cheese and your choice of topping. Bake on the bottom rack of a 475°F (240°C) oven for about 12 minutes.

A precooked flatbread, pizza base or focaccia bread will take less time, 8-10 minutes.

It is not necessary to measure pizza ingredients accurately. Use what you like and what you have on hand. For a crisp crust and tasty roasted vegetables, don't overload the pizza shell. For variety and convenience, even split English muffins or whole-wheat hamburger buns can be used as a pizza base.

Here are some combinations to add to the sauce and cheese:

Mushroom Pizza

Add 1 cup (250 mL) thinly sliced mushrooms, 1 small red onion and 3 Roma tomatoes, thinly sliced. Sprinkle a little more cheese on top. Bake as above.

Pepperoni and Cheese Pizza

Add 8 oz. (250 g) thinly sliced pepperoni, 4 thinly sliced Roma tomatoes and 1 cup (250 mL) of a second cheese such as grated Asiago or Cheddar and a sprinkling of dried Italian seasoning. Bake as above.

Pizza is a circle of thin dough covered with a topping and baked. Make your own pizza base or buy a ready-made crust, fresh or frozen, from the supermarket.

For alternate pizza bases, try English muffins. Split them, lightly toast and top them, toast again. Pita breads can be split, toasted and topped, too. Make pizza boats from French bread cut length-wise and topped. Brush a bakery flatbread with olive oil and add toppings. For a delicious thin-crust pizza, use a tortilla as the base.

Here are ideas for quick pizza toppings and recipes for 2 favorites.

Garden Tomato and Basil Pizza

Layer slices of fresh garden tomatoes on prepared pizza crust. Add ¼ cup (60 mL) chopped fresh basil. Top with 1 cup (250 mL) of grated cheese. Bake as on page 25.

Broccoli, Tomato and Cottage Cheese Pizza

In a bowl, mix ½ cup (125 mL) of drained, low-fat cottage cheese, ½ cup (125 mL) chopped broccoli florets and 2 chopped Roma tomatoes. Spread over pizza shell and top with 1 cup (250 mL) of grated sharp Cheddar or feta cheese. Bake as on page 25.

Shrimp Pizza

Spread a pizza crust with pesto sauce instead of the tomato sauce and cheese. Rinse and drain a can of broken or salad shrimp and mix with 3-4 chopped Roma tomatoes and 1 cup (250 mL) of crumbled feta cheese. Spread over the pizza. Bake as on page 25.

Mediterranean Pizza

Spread a large pizza shell with ¼ cup (60 mL) of pesto instead of the tomato sauce and cheese. Add a seeded and thinly sliced red pepper, a small, chopped red onion, 2 chopped Roma tomatoes, ¼ cup (60 mL) sliced black Greek olives and ½ cup (125 mL) crumbled feta cheese. Top with ¼ cup (60 mL) of toasted pine nuts. Bake as on page 25.

Spinach and Feta Pizza

Brush a pizza crust with olive oil instead of the tomato sauce and cheese. Distribute chopped spinach (a 10 oz. [285 g] pkg. thawed, squeezed dry) over crust. Sprinkle 8 oz. (250 g) of crumbled plain feta or basil and sun-dried tomato feta over the pizza crust. Add ¼ cup (60 mL) of chopped black Greek olives and sprinkle with crumbled dried oregano, salt and freshly ground pepper to taste. Bake as on page 25.

TIP: Serving these pizzas means you don't have to cope with that enormous take-home box that never fits in the garbage can.

TIP: To keep ready-grated cheeses fresh after opening, keep them in freezer bags in the freezer.

Pizza with Feta, Tomatoes and Shrimp

Adult flavors in an easy-make pizza. So good!

1	large baked pizza bread shell OR focaccia	1
¼ cup	bottled pesto sauce	60 mL
4 oz.	feta cheese, crumbled	115 g
16	Kalamata olives, pitted and halved	16
½ cup	chopped red onion	125 mL
4	Roma tomatoes, chopped	4
8 oz.	mozzarella cheese, grated	250 g
2x4 oz.	cans shrimp, drained OR 8 oz. (250 g) frozen shrimp, thawed and blotted dry	2x113 g

- Preheat oven to 450°F (230°C).

- Place bread shell on pizza pan and spread with pesto sauce.

- Sprinkle with the rest of the ingredients, except shrimp. Be creative in your arrangement, if you have time.

- Bake for 10 minutes. Remove from oven and arrange shrimp on top.

- Return to oven and bake 3-5 minutes more, until cheese melts.

TIP: To pit olives easily, put them on a chopping block and press down firmly with the flat of a large knife. The olive will compress and the pit will be released.

Variation:

For **Pepperoni Pizza**, top pizza base with:

½ cup	pizza sauce	125 mL
½ tsp.	dried red pepper flakes.	2 mL
8 ozs.	pizza cheese, grated (2 cups [250 mL])	250 g
3 ozs.	pepperoni, thinly sliced	85 g
4	Roma tomatoes, thinly sliced	4

Combine sauce and pepper flakes; spread over base and top with remaining ingredients. Bake at 450°F (230°C) for 12-15 minutes, until cheese is melted.

I like the small cans of pasta sauce for quick pizzas and small servings of pasta. Then I am not committed to using up that big jar in the fridge.

WRAPS, TORTILLAS & PITA POCKETS

Wraps are pliable flatbreads or tortillas intended for meat, vegetable, egg or cheese fillings. They can be as creative as you wish or they can be made from what is on hand or in the fridge. They go well with soups or salads. Eat as is or microwave for 20-30 seconds.

Wraps are good for snacks and lunches and complement soups and salads. They pack and travel well for picnics and boating trips. Choose any of your favorite sandwich combos, layer a wrap, roll neatly and serve.

Cold wraps cut best when wrapped in plastic and stored in the fridge for an hour.

Quick Wraps

Pita pockets, buns and tortillas make suitcase sandwiches. To heat a single pita or tortilla, microwave on high for 30 seconds.

For a melt, split a bun or English muffin, top with a filling and sliced cheese. Grill in the oven for a few minutes, until the cheese melts.

Put a little cheese and salsa on half a tortilla and fold it over. Heat in the microwave for 30 seconds or in a frying pan for 1-2 minutes each side. Lunch is ready! Adding cooked chicken, beef or mashed black beans makes a meal.

Many of your favorite sandwich combinations can be served in a wrap. For a change, try one of these combos:

- For a **Carrot and Raisin Wrap**, spread an 8 or 9" (20 or 23 cm) tortilla with cream cheese or sprinkle with grated Cheddar. Layer with grated carrot, a few sultanas and chopped celery. Sprinkle with salt and pepper. Roll, wrap in plastic until ready to eat. Cut in thirds. *Pictured on page 35.*

- To cream cheese base, add leftover chicken or deli fajita chicken, chopped lettuce and walnuts, mayonnaise, salt and pepper.

- To cream cheese base, add sliced ham, sliced mushrooms, spinach leaves or lettuce, creamy mustard and mayonnaise.

- To cream cheese base, on a whole-wheat or pesto tortilla, add Dijon mustard, sliced roast beef and thin cucumber slices.

Tuna Salad Wraps

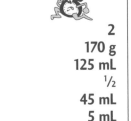

2	large tortillas	2
6 oz.	can water-packed tuna, drained	170 g
½ cup	diced celery (2 stalks)	125 mL
½	red pepper, seeded and finely diced	½
3 tbsp.	mayonnaise	45 mL
1 tsp.	lemon juice	5 mL
½ tsp.	curry powder (optional)	2 mL
	salt and pepper to taste	
	shredded lettuce (optional)	

- In a medium bowl, flake tuna. Add remaining ingredients, except lettuce, and mix well. Spread over the tortillas; add lettuce if using. Roll up.

- Serve at room temperature or heat in microwave for 30 seconds. Cut in halves or thirds to serve.

Makes 2 tortillas, 6 or 9 pieces

Variation: Omit the curry and add 1 cup (250 mL) grated cheese and/or chopped green onions, green pepper, grated carrots and lettuce.

Variation: For **Salmon Salad Wraps**, **Egg Salad** or **Chicken Salad Wraps**, substitute salmon, chopped hard-boiled eggs or chicken chunks or flakes for the tuna. Omit the curry if you prefer.

Variation: For **Chili Wraps**, put leftover chili and grated cheese on each tortilla. Turn the sides in; roll; heat and cut in half to serve.

Pictured on page 35.

Ham and Cheese Wraps

4	10" (25 cm) tortillas	4
	creamy mustard OR Dijon and mayonnaise mixed	
8	slices EACH ham and cheese	8
2	tomatoes, thinly sliced	2

- Spread each tortilla lightly with the mustard mixture. Layer with ham, cheese and tomato slices.

- Roll up. Serve at room temperature or heat in a microwave for 30 seconds. Cut in half to serve.

Serves 4

Variations: For **Chicken and Cheese Wraps** or **Roast Beef and Cheese Wraps**, substitute sliced deli roast chicken or beef for the ham.

Chicken Pita with Alfalfa Sprouts

Good things on top of or in bread make quick meals.

1 cup	flaked or diced cooked chicken	250 mL
½ cup	chopped celery	125 mL
½ cup	drained, chopped water chestnuts	125 mL
2	oranges, peeled, sectioned and chopped	2
¼ cup	mayonnaise OR mayonnaise and yogurt	60 mL
2 tsp.	soy sauce	10 mL
5 oz.	alfalfa sprouts, rinsed and dried with a paper towel – use what you need	140 g
½ cup	thin cucumber slices	125 mL
3	7" (18 cm) pitas, halved and opened to form pockets	3

- In a medium bowl, combine chicken, celery, water chestnuts, orange, mayonnaise and soy sauce.

- Line bottom of each pita half with sprouts, add chicken mixture, cucumber and more sprouts. Serve.

Serves 3-6

Variation: This can also be a **Tuna Pita**. Substitute a 6 oz. (170 g) can of water-packed tuna, drained, for the chicken.

Variation: For a **Chicken Pita from the Pantry**, use a 6½ oz. (184 g) can of chicken, drained and flaked.

TIP: Leftover sprouts can be added to salads and sandwiches or top a burger.

Pictured on page 35.

Curried Chicken Pita Pockets

Chicken, vegetables and fruit in pita pockets.

1 cup	diced cooked chicken	250 mL
½	apple, finely chopped	½
¼ cup	raisins, washed and dried	60 mL
1	celery stalk, finely chopped	1
1	green onion, thinly sliced, use most of the green	1
2 tbsp.	mayonnaise	30 mL
2 tbsp.	yogurt	30 mL
1 tsp.	curry powder	5 mL
	salt and pepper	
	chopped lettuce	
4	whole-wheat pitas, cut in half and opened to form pockets	4

- In a medium-sized bowl, combine chicken, apple, raisins, celery and onion.

- Combine mayonnaise, yogurt, curry powder and a little salt and pepper. Stir into chicken mixture.

- Line the bottom of each pita half with lettuce; add a spoonful of chicken mixture and more lettuce. Serve.

Serves 4-6

Variation: Add 2-3 tbsp. (30-45 mL) of mango chutney to the chicken mixture or serve the chutney on the side.

TIP: For a starter, stuff tiny pita pocket halves.

Tuna Salad Bunwiches or Melts

Make a sandwich, bunwich or melt.

6 oz.	can water-packed tuna, drained	184 g
1/2 cup	diced celery	125 mL
1/4 cup	mayonnaise	60 mL
1 tsp.	lemon juice	5 mL
1/2	red pepper, seeded and diced	1/2
3-4	sandwich buns	3-4
	lettuce, tomato, cucumber	

- Break up tuna and mix with the celery, mayonnaise, lemon juice and peppers.
- Divide tuna mixture among buns; add lettuce, slices of tomatoes and cucumbers and serve.

Serves 3-4

Variation: Add small cubes of Monterey Jack cheese, chopped green onions or black olives.

Variation: For a main-dish salad, serve a portion of the tuna mixture on a plate of mixed greens with tomato and cucumber slices on the side.

Variation: Put lettuce in half a pita pocket, add tuna salad and more lettuce and cucumber slices. Serve.

Variation: For a **Tuna Melt**, spread tuna mixture on English muffin halves or hamburger buns; top with sliced cheese and bake at 400°F (200°C) until the cheese melts, about 8 minutes.

TIP: A toaster oven makes great melts. No need to heat the oven in your stove.

Chicken Bunwiches

Use a barbecue or stove-top grill to make chicken breast burgers. Make a salad with pre-washed greens and orange slices and your meal is ready.

2	boneless, skinless chicken breasts	2
1 tsp.	vegetable oil	5 mL
	salt and pepper OR seasoning salt	
4	hamburger buns	4
	butter OR margarine OR mustard mayonnaise	
	lettuce, tomato and/or cucumber slices	

- Using a meat mallet or the heel of your hand, flatten the chicken breasts between 2 pieces of plastic wrap or in a plastic bag.

- Brush with oil and sprinkle with salt and pepper or seasoning salt.

- Cook on a greased grill or barbecue over medium-high heat, turning once until no longer pink, about 10 minutes. Reduce heat if pan seems too hot.

- Transfer to a cutting board and let cool slightly. Cut each breast in half horizontally.

- Heat split buns on the grill; spread with butter OR mustard mayonnaise spread.

- Top with chicken, lettuce, tomato and cucumber.

4 servings

Variation: For **Chutney Chicken Bunwiches**, brush 4 red onion and 4 red pepper slices with oil; grill or barbecue just until heated through. Add to the chicken bunwiches with 1 tbsp. (15 mL) of chutney.

Quesadillas

A quesadilla is a Tex-Mex grilled cheese sandwich. Hefty versions are good for a meal with a bowl of soup or a salad. Small tortillas, filled and folded and cut into slices, make great starters. Serve with sour cream and salsa.

To assemble Quesadillas
- Heat a large, non-stick frying pan on medium-high heat.
- Lay a 10" (25 cm) tortilla on the counter. Cover half with filling. Fold the uncovered half over the filling.
- Transfer to a frying pan and cook until golden, turning once, about 2 minutes per side.

Cheese Quesadilla
- Spread half the tortilla with processed cheese spread; sprinkle with $1/2$ cup (125 mL) grated mozzarella cheese. Fold and cook.

Cheese, Tomato and Onion Quesadilla
- Spread half the tortilla with cheese spread. Top with 2 Roma tomatoes, chopped and 1 green onion, chopped. Fold and cook.

Italian Quesadilla
- Spread half the tortilla with chunky pasta sauce. Top with a few slices of salami cut in strips, $1/2$ tsp. (2 mL) basil and $1/2$ cup (125 mL) grated cheese. Fold and cook.

Swiss Quesadilla
- Cover half the tortilla with creamy mustard blend, 1 slice of deli ham cut in strips and $1/2$ cup (125 mL) grated Swiss cheese. Fold and cook.

Tex-Mex Quesadilla
- Spread half the tortilla with refried beans. Top with grated cheese, a little chopped jalapeño and chopped green onions. Fold and cook.

Tomato, Feta and Pesto
- Crumble 4 oz. (115 g) of feta cheese; add 2 Roma tomatoes, chopped, 1 tbsp. (15 mL) of sliced black olives and 1 tbsp. (15 mL) of pesto. Mix and spread on half of a 10" (25 cm) tortilla. Fold and cook.

Chili Quesadillas (leftover or canned)
- Using leftover or canned chili, allow about $1/2$ cup (125 mL) chili for half of a tortilla. Sprinkle with Cheddar and chopped jalapeños if you like. Fold and cook.

TIP: Quesadillas can be heated on a barbecue or on a stove-top grill. If grilling, brush or spray the grill with vegetable oil.

WRAPS, PITA POCKET, SALADS

Chicken Quesadillas

This is a good way to use the chicken left over from the deli dinner or last night's barbecue.

8	7" (18 cm) tortillas	8
½ cup	tomato sauce OR mild salsa	125 mL
1 cup	shredded or diced cooked chicken	250 mL
1½ cups	grated mozzarella OR Cheddar cheese	375 mL
½ cup	chopped green pepper	125 mL
1 tbsp.	vegetable oil	15 mL

- Heat oven to 375°F (190°C).
- Cover a cookie sheet with parchment paper and arrange 4 tortillas on top.
- Spread 2 tbsp. (30 mL) of sauce on each tortilla.
- Divide the chicken, cheese and green pepper among the tortillas and spread to the edge.
- Top each with a second tortilla. Brush with oil.
- Bake until heated through, 6-8 minutes.
- Cut into 4 wedges and serve with sour cream and salsa.

Serves 4

Microwave method: Place 2 tortillas on paper towel and microwave on medium for 2 minutes, or until tortillas are warmed and cheese melted.

Variation: For **Beef Quesadillas**, cook 8 oz. (250 g) lean ground beef until meat changes color. Drain and pat with a paper towel to remove all the fat. Add 1 small onion, chopped; 1 tbsp. (15 mL) chili powder; 1 cup (250 mL) tomato sauce. Stir and heat. Spread over 4 quesadillas; top with Cheddar cheese and a second tortilla. Brush with oil and bake as above. Serve with salsa and sour cream.

POTATOES

I love potatoes but don't have the patience to remove the cooked potato from the skin, mash it, cheese it and return it to the skin. I do like potatoes topped so that the veggies, sauce or cheese enhance the potato texture and flavor and provide a main dish for supper. Here are 2 methods for cooking the potatoes and topping ideas to go with them.

Baked Potatoes

Oven method

4	medium, oblong-shaped baking potatoes,	4

- Scrub the potatoes; prick with a fork or knife-point in several places. Bake at 400°F (200°C) for 45 minutes, or until potato begins to soften. Squeeze the potatoes with your thumb and finger to check.

Microwave method

- For 1 large potato, scrub and prick well; cook on high for 4-5 minutes. Wrap in a kitchen towel to continue cooking and keep warm.

- For 4 potatoes, arrange in a circle in the microwave, about 1" (2.5 cm) apart. Cook on high for 10-13 minutes, turning halfway through cooking time. Wrap in a kitchen towel and let stand 5 minutes to continue cooking.

SERVING IDEAS: Serve baked potatoes with your choice of toppings or use in soup or vegetable dishes when cooked potato is called for. To make tasty **Hash Browns**, *second-day potatoes can be cut up and heated in a non-stick pan with 1 tbsp. (15 mL) of oil and some chopped onions, or use them in a frittata.*

Baked Potatoes Topped with Meat and Veggies

Hearty and quick when made with microwave-baked potatoes.

4	medium baking potatoes (Russets, Gems or Yukon Gold)	4
½ lb.	lean ground beef	250 g
10 oz.	can ready-to-serve chunky vegetable soup	284 mL
1½ tbsp.	flour	22 mL
1-2 cups	grated cheese	250-500 mL

- Cook the potatoes in the microwave, about 12 minutes for 4 potatoes. Turn over part way through the cooking time and wrap in a kitchen towel when cooked but still firm.

- While the potatoes are cooking, spray a non-stick pan with cooking spray and heat on medium-high. Cook the meat until done, about 5 minutes. Using a wooden or nylon spatula, break the meat into small pieces.

- When the meat is cooked and lightly browned, drain and blot with a paper towel to absorb extra fat.

- Add the flour to the soup. Mix thoroughly with a fork. Add the soup to the pan. Heat and stir until bubbly.

- Cut the potatoes halfway through, lengthwise. Squeeze to mash and open the potato.

- Serve potatoes topped with the meat mixture and grated cheese.

Serves 4

Variation: For a change, prepared potatoes can be topped with tuna salad and cheese. Broil in the oven or toaster oven until the cheese melts.

Baked Potato and Toppers

Your choice of topping makes the baked potato a side dish or a meal. Cut baked potatoes about 1" (2.5 cm) deep from end to end. Gently push the sides to release the roasted potato. Protect your finger tips with pot holders or a tea towel. Serve with a topping.

Tuna Topper

6.5 oz.	can tuna, water-packed, drained and flaked	184 g
¼ cup	chopped celery	60 mL
1	green onion, chopped (top too)	1
½	tomato, chopped	½
¼ cup	light mayonnaise (try half yogurt)	60 mL
½ tsp.	curry powder	2 mL
	salt and pepper to taste	

• Combine all ingredients and divide among 4 split baked potatoes.

Serves 4

Variation: For a change, top tuna mixture with cheese slices or grated cheese. Broil in the oven or toaster oven until the cheese melts.

Chili and Cheese Topper

19 oz.	can chili OR 2 cups (500 mL) leftover chili	540 mL
1 cup	grated Cheddar cheese	250 mL

• Heat the chili in a pot or in the microwave. Spoon over 4 split baked potatoes and top with cheese. For bigger appetites use more chili.

TIP: A pull-top 7½ oz. (212 g) can of chili, heated, makes a topping for a single potato. Sprinkle with grated Cheddar cheese.

Serves 4

Broccoli and Cottage Cheese Topper

This is a good meal for one, especially when you are too tired to cook.

½ cup	cottage cheese	125 mL
½ cup	cooked, peeled, diced broccoli	125 mL
1	green onion, sliced	1
	salt and pepper to taste	

• Combine the cottage cheese, broccoli and onion. Top a split baked potato. For 4 servings, use 1½ cups (375 mL) of cottage cheese, 1½ cups (375 mL) of diced broccoli and 4 green onions.

Serves 1

Cottage Cheese, Green Onions, Cucumber Topper

1 cup	low-fat cottage cheese	250 mL
1/4 cup	sour cream	60 mL
2	green onions, chopped	2
1/4 cup	seeded, chopped cucumber	60 mL
	salt and pepper to taste	

- Mix cottage cheese with sour cream, green onions and cucumber. Sprinkle with a little salt and pepper. Serve on 2 split potatoes.

Serves 2

Broccoli Cheddar Sauce

This is a quick and satisfying combination of flavors.

1/2 x 10 oz.	can broccoli Cheddar soup	1/2 x 284 mL
1/4 cup	milk OR cream	60 mL
1/4 cup	grated Cheddar cheese	60 mL
	pepper to taste	

- Heat soup, milk and cheese. Add a little pepper and serve over 2 large, split baked potatoes.

Serves 2 or serves 4 as a side dish

Broccoli & Cheddar Topper for One

1	single serving instant soup, broccoli, cauliflower or vegetable	1
1/2 cup	milk	125 mL
1/2 cup	chopped broccoli	125 mL
1/4 cup	grated Cheddar cheese	60 mL
	pepper to taste	

- Combine soup, milk and broccoli in a 1 cup (250 mL) measure. Microwave on high for 2 minutes, stirring occasionally. Add a little pepper. Spoon onto a split baked potato; top with grated cheese and serve.

SUPER-QUICK MEALS & SNACKS

10-minute chicken, beef, egg and tofu dishes

We need super-quick meal ideas and recipes when we are hungry and have no time to search for a recipe to prepare a meal, or when we just can't face the kitchen . . . again.

Some of these super-quick recipes use convenience food products to create meals that are as quick as fast food pickups – but much healthier.

There are super-quick meals throughout this book. This section is in addition to those meals and is the result of talking with the busy cooks in my family. It is meant to be a handy resource and the goal is to keep the food preparation simple and stress free.

Be sure to consider the dishes in the Lunches and Light Meals section, see page 19. Choose a pizza, a wrap, a quesadilla or a topped potato.

Grill a chicken breast, see page 111, and make a burger with lettuce, tomato and red and yellow pepper strips.

Choose eggs and make an omelet, see page 48, or eggs and vegetables and make a frittata, see page 47. Add a salad and a chunky bread and the meal is ready.

When you have the basics in your store cupboard and fridge you will always be able to have a satisfying meal ready in minutes.

Improvise, top it, stuff it, or sauce it! Try some of these.

Sorta pizza

Cover a tortilla or English muffin half with tomato sauce and grated cheese. Heat at 450°F (230°C) for 6-8 minutes. Add wiener, pepperoni or smokie slices, ham or shrimp if you have them. Prepare as many as you need or can eat.

Tuna Burger

Drain a 6½ oz. (184 g) can of water-packed tuna. Flake and mix with 1 egg, ¼ cup (60 mL) of fine bread or cracker crumbs, ¼ cup (60 mL) yogurt or mayonnaise, 1 tsp. (5 mL) curry powder and a little salt and pepper. Shape into 2 or 3 patties. Cook in a non-stick pan over medium heat until heated through and lightly browned. Serve in a bun with lettuce, tomato and cucumber and a little chutney or mayonnaise.

Serves 2-3

Chicken Quesadilla

Drain and flake a 6½ oz. (184 g) can of chicken. Mix lightly with 1 cup (250 mL) grated Mozzarella or Cheddar and ¼ cup (60 mL) of salsa. Select 3 large (8-10″ [20-25 cm]) tortillas. Spread ⅓ of chicken mixture on half of each tortilla. Fold in half and press edges together. Heat a light oil in a non-stick pan over medium heat. Add quesadilla and cook on each side until lightly browned and cheese is melting, 2-3 minutes each side. Cut into wedges and serve with salsa and sour cream. To cook on the barbecue or on a grilling pan, brush the outside of the tortilla with oil and grill for a few minutes.

Pasta and Cheese

Cook 4 oz. (115 g) (2-3 servings) spaghetti, drain and toss with 2 tbsp. (30 mL) butter or olive oil and ½ cup (125 mL) chopped fresh herbs or 2 tsp. (10 mL) dried Italian herbs. Add 1 cup (250 mL) grated sharp Cheddar or Asiago cheese and toss again. Serve with salad greens or sliced tomatoes and crusty bread.

Pasta and Spicy Tomato Sauce

Sauté red pepper flakes in a little olive oil. Add chopped onion and minced garlic if you like. Add a can of diced tomatoes; heat and toss with hot, cooked pasta. Sprinkle with grated Parmesan or Romano cheese.

Pasta and Pesto

Toss hot, cooked pasta with bottled pesto sauce to taste. Sprinkle with freshly grated Parmesan, salt and freshly ground pepper. Serve with sliced deli meats or chicken and a salad of prewashed greens and sliced tomatoes.

Hearty Hamburger Soup

Sometimes I prepare this soup while I am cooking an oven meal or tidying up the kitchen. That way I have bonus meals on hand.

½ lb.	lean ground beef	250 g
28 oz.	can stewed tomatoes	796 mL
5 cups	beef broth OR water	1.25 L
3 cups	frozen Italian OR stir-fry vegetables, partially thawed and chopped into bite-sized pieces	750 mL
1½ oz.	pkg. dried onion soup mix	40 g

- In a large saucepan, cook beef until it changes color and is lightly browned. Drain and blot with a paper towel to remove excess fat.
- Add the remaining ingredients, bring to a boil. Reduce heat; cover and simmer for 10-15 minutes. Serve with garlic breadsticks. Freeze any remaining soup for another meal.

Serves 6-8

Variation: Add 1 cup (250 mL) water or broth and 1 cup (250 mL) small pasta with the vegetables. If soup is too thick, add more broth or water.

TIP: Add chopped leftover vegetables, salad and rice or pasta.

Sloppy Joes

Sloppy Joes are a standby in most households; now try them with turkey.

1 lb.	lean ground beef OR turkey	500 g
1	onion, diced	1
½ cup	ketchup	125 mL
2 tbsp.	chili sauce	30 mL
½ tsp.	dry mustard	2 mL
1 tsp.	cider vinegar	5 mL
1 tbsp.	brown sugar	15 mL
6	whole-wheat buns	6

- Spray a large, non-stick pan with cooking spray or oil. Heat over medium-high heat. Add meat and onions; cook until meat changes color and begins to brown. Pour off fat and blot meat with a paper towel to remove additional fat.
- Add the remaining ingredients, except buns. Mix well and heat until bubbly. Reduce heat, cover and cook for 10-20 minutes. Serve in buns.

Serves 6

TIP: Leftovers make a good sandwich filling or baked potato topping.

Pizza Boats

This is a family favorite and probably the most often-served recipe at our house. Pizza Boats don't need a structured recipe, just a little tomato sauce and whatever you have on hand. They are good with soup or salad. The addition of cooked ground meat makes a meal for 2 or 3.

1	loaf French bread, 15" (38 cm)	1
½-1 cup	cheese spread	125-250 mL
1 cup	pasta sauce (your choice)	250 mL
1 tsp.	dried oregano OR Italian spice	5 mL
1 cup	grated pizza cheese	250 mL

- Heat oven to 400°F (200°C).

- Cut bread in half lengthwise, place on a cookie sheet and spread with cheese spread.

- Lightly cover with pasta sauce, cheese and oregano.

- Bake until cheese has melted and bread is toasted, about 15 minutes.

Variation: Top the cheese spread with thin slices of salami and tomato before you add the tomato sauce and grated cheese.

Variation: Brown ½ lb. (250 g) of ground meat and 1 cup (250 mL) chopped onion. Drain and blot with paper towel to remove fat. Add to the cheese spread and top with a few thin tomato slices.

TIP: Anything goes. Make your pizza boat of choice.

5 in 10 Chili

Five ingredients make a chili in 10 minutes. Use **chili-style** *red kidney beans.*

1	**EACH onion AND green pepper, chopped**	1
14 oz.	**can red kidney beans, chili-style**	398 mL
14 oz.	**can diced tomatoes**	398 mL
1/3 cup	**instant rice**	75 mL

- Combine all ingredients in a large saucepan over high heat. Bring to a boil, reduce heat and simmer for 8-10 minutes.

Variation: Garnish with chopped green onions and grated Cheddar.

Variation: Add 8 oz. (250 g) precooked ground meat.

TIP: *For more servings, add a second can of drained beans.*

TIP: *Chili lovers add a tbsp. (15 mL) of chili powder, cayenne or hot sauce to taste.*

Black Bean Quesadillas

A quick supper by itself or with soup or salad.

15 oz.	**can black beans, rinsed and drained**	425 mL
1 cup	**shredded Cheddar OR mozzarella cheese**	250 mL
1 tbsp.	**chili powder**	15 mL
8	**6" (15 cm) tortillas**	8
	salsa and sour cream	

- In a bowl, crush the beans a little. Add the cheese and chili powder and mix well.

- Spread the bean mixture on 4 tortillas. Top with the remaining 4 tortillas. Now it's a quesadilla.

- Cook quesadillas on both sides in a non-stick skillet over medium heat, until heated through, about 3 minutes on each side. Cut each in 4 pieces and serve with salsa and sour cream.

Serves 4

Variation: Use the same method with other ingredients. Try cooked chicken with green peppers, chili powder and cheese. Try an all vegetable combo with chili powder and 1-2 cups (250-500 mL) of grated cheese.

TIP: *For extra-quick cooking, use 2 pans.*

Vegetable Frittata

A little more substantial than an omelet, the eggs are finished in the oven; no folding is needed.

1 tbsp.	vegetable oil	15 mL
1	small onion, chopped	1
1-2 cups	chopped vegetables, such as red or green pepper, broccoli, mushrooms, zucchini, tomatoes	250-500 mL
	salt and pepper to taste	
6	eggs	6
1 cup	grated mozzarella OR Cheddar cheese	250 mL
1 tsp.	dried basil or 2 tbsp. (30 mL) chopped fresh	5 mL

- Heat oil in a large non-stick skillet over medium-high heat. Tip pan to evenly coat the bottom.

- Add onion and cook for 2 minutes. Add the vegetables of your choice. Cook and stir until tender, about 3 minutes. Sprinkle with salt and pepper.

- Whisk eggs, cheese and basil in a small bowl and pour over vegetable mixture. Stir.

- Cook, lifting edges gently with a spatula so that the egg mixture combines with the veggies and flows to the bottom of the pan. Turn the broiler on about now.

- Continue to cook until the edges are set and the bottom is brown (lift with a spatula to look), about 5 minutes.

- Wrap pan handle with foil if it is not ovenproof. Place the frittata under the broiler until the top is set and lightly browned, about 2 minutes.

- Run a knife around the edge of the pan to loosen. Slide frittata onto a serving platter or cut in 4 and serve from the pan.

Serves 4

Variation: For a **Quick Potato Frittata**, substitute 4 cups (1 L) diced cooked potatoes or frozen hash browns and 4 chopped green onions, for the onion and other vegetables. Cook the potatoes until browned, 4-5 minutes; add the green onions to the egg mixture, omitting the basil, and proceed with the recipe.

Tomato Cheese Omelet

Breakfast for dinner – if you have 3 eggs, a little cheese and a vegetable, you have dinner for 2.

3	large eggs	3
2 tbsp.	water	30 mL
1 tsp.	butter OR vegetable oil	5 mL
1	large tomato, chopped (use 2 or 3 Romas if you wish)	1
1 cup	shredded Cheddar OR mozzarella cheese salt and pepper to taste	250 mL

- Whisk eggs and water in a small bowl.

- In a large, non-stick skillet, heat oil over medium heat. Tip pan to evenly coat the bottom. Add eggs to pan. Reduce heat a little. Cook eggs until beginning to set. Gently lift edges and tilt pan so that uncooked egg runs under the omelet.

- When egg is almost set, sprinkle half of the omelet with tomatoes and cheese.

- With a large spatula, turn the other half of the omelet onto the egg and tomato side. Cook for about 2 minutes, until cheese is melted and tomato warmed.

- Cut omelet in half and serve with a green salad and toast.

Serves 2

Variation: There are endless combinations. Try:
- Drop 4 small spoonfuls of herb and garlic cream cheese and 2 tbsp. (30 mL) of salsa on half of the omelet in place of the tomato and cheese.

- Chopped ham and grated cheese.

- Sautéed mushrooms OR sautéed zucchini and tomato AND sautéed onion with any of the above.

TIP: To make perfect omelets quickly, stick to the 3-egg size and make as many as you need. To make a larger omelet, increase the eggs to 6, the water to ¼ cup (60 mL) and cooking time as needed. Use a larger pan if you have it.

TIP: For a classy presentation, sprinkle the folded omelet with grated cheese; broil until cheese is melted and lightly browned.

Tortellini with Tomatoes and Zucchini

This is a super-quick meal. It is good with a green salad.

9 oz.	pkg. cheese tortellini	280 g
1 tbsp.	olive OR vegetable oil	15 mL
2	garlic cloves, minced or 1 tsp. (5 mL) bottled minced garlic	2
2	small zucchini, quartered lengthwise and cut into ½" (1.3 cm) slices	2
14 oz. can	diced tomatoes	398 mL
½ cup	chicken broth, vegetable broth OR water	125 mL
1 tsp.	dried basil or 2 tbsp. (30 mL) chopped fresh	5 mL
	salt and pepper to taste	

- Cook tortellini in a large pot of boiling water until tender, 5-7 minutes. See package directions.

- Meanwhile, heat oil in a large, non-stick pan over medium-high heat. Add garlic and zucchini; cook and stir for 5 minutes,

- Add tomatoes, broth and basil. Cook and stir for 5 minutes. Pour sauce over drained tortellini and serve.

Serves 2-3

Variation: For a quicker supper, cook tortellini as directed. Heat 3 cups (750 mL) of spaghetti sauce and pour over tortellini. Serve with a salad and crusty bread.

Look for flavoured canned chicken and beef broths – oriental, tomato and basil, and so on. There are several new products that can be used as quick sauces for meat and pasta dishes.

5-Minute Sweet and Sour Tofu Stir-Fry

This recipe is from Brita Housez. In Tofu Mania *Brita demystifies tofu and gives us dozens of ways to incorporate tofu in all our meals and baking.*

2 tbsp.	vegetable oil	30 ml
1	medium onion, coarsely chopped	1
1	red pepper, julienned	1
½	green pepper, julienned	½
1 lb.	medium or firm tofu, cut into bite-sized pieces*	500 g
	salt and pepper to taste	
16 oz.	jar sweet and sour sauce (or recipe below)	455 mL

- Over high heat, in a wok or deep, frying pan, heat oil.

- Add onions and peppers and stir-fry 2 minutes. Add tofu and continue to stir-fry 1 minute.

- Sprinkle with salt and pepper. Fold in sweet and sour sauce. Reduce heat to medium and cook until heated through.

- Serve over rice or Chinese noodles.

Serves 4

* If your family is not tofu friendly, try grating or crumbling the tofu. It will disappear into the vegetable mixture.

Variations: For **Hawaiian Chicken** or **Pork**, just add thin strips of stir-fried chicken or pork to the above stir-fry and sauce. Yummy! Also, try shrimp or any firm-fleshed white fish, such as cod or halibut.

Basic Sweet and Sour Sauce

¼-½ cup	white vinegar	60-125 mL
½ cup	brown sugar	125 mL
½ cup	ketchup	125 mL
8 oz.	can pineapple tidbits with juice	227 mL
2 tsp.	cornstarch	10 mL

- In a medium saucepan, combine all ingredients. Over medium heat, stir until mixture comes to a boil.

- Add desired quantity of sauce to sautéed vegetables, tofu and/or meat. Cover and refrigerate leftover sauce for up to 1 week.

Salmon Patties

An old-fashioned favorite – good nutrition and great flavor.

15 oz.	can salmon	418 g
2	green onions, chopped (use most of the green part)	2
½ cup	dry bread crumbs (seasoned or plain)	125 mL
1	egg	1
2-3 tbsp.	vegetable oil	30-45 mL

- Drain the salmon; place in a bowl and flake with a fork. Thinly slice the green onions and add them to the salmon along with 2 tbsp. (30 mL) of the bread crumbs and the egg. Mix to blend well.

- Form salmon mixture into 6 oval patties, ½-¾" (1.3-2 cm) thick. Dip the patties in the remaining bread crumbs to coat.

- Heat oil in a large, non-stick skillet over medium heat. Add the salmon patties and cook, turning once, until both sides are crisp and golden and the patties are heated through, about 7 minutes total.

- Serve with lemon wedges or Lemon Pepper sauce, below.

Serves 3

Lemon Pepper Sauce

½ cup	sour cream	125 mL
1 tsp.	lemon juice	5 mL
1 tsp.	lemon pepper OR citrus pepper seasoning (NO SALT ADDED VERSION)	5 mL
⅛ tsp.	salt	0.5 mL
1 tbsp.	chopped fresh parsley (optional)	15 mL

In a small bowl, combine all of the ingredients. Cover and refrigerate until needed.

Quick Chicken Dinner – Deli Style

Use this meal idea when you bring a rotisserie chicken home from the deli.

1	cooked deli chicken	1
4 cups	lettuce/mixed greens	1 L
1	large tomato, sliced	1
½	cucumber, sliced	½
	bottled dressing of your choice	

- Cut the chicken into serving-sized pieces. Cut the breasts from the carcass, cut the legs from the backbone, cut again at the joint to make 4 pieces. Arrange chicken pieces on a platter of greens.

- Add sliced tomatoes and cucumbers.

- Pass the salad dressing. Serve with rice or deli potato salad.

Serves 4

TIP: *When the meal is finished, strip the bones of meat, add any leftovers from dinner, refrigerate. The next day make a* **Chicken Quesadilla**, *see page 37, or chop the chicken, add a little low-fat mayonnaise and diced celery, and you have* **Chicken Salad** *for a sandwich filling or a salad topping.*

SECRET: *Don't put the stripped carcass in the fridge. For some reason it just stays there and annoys you every time you open the door.*

Sorta Barbecued Chicken

Add a little chutney to bottled barbecue sauce for a quick chicken with a new flavor. Serve it in buns and pass the carrot and celery sticks.

¾-1 lb.	boneless, skinless chicken breasts or thighs	340-500 g
	vegetable oil or spray	
¼ cup	bottled barbecue sauce	60 mL
¼ cup	chutney, mango or other	60 mL

Sorta Barbecued Chicken *continued*

- Cut chicken into bite-sized pieces.

- Spray a large, non-stick pan with cooking spray or oil. Heat on medium-high. Add chicken; cook and stir until chicken is tender and no pink color remains in the meat, about 4 minutes.

- Stir in barbecue sauce and chutney. Cook and stir until heated through, about 3 minutes. Serve in buns or with rice and salad.

Serves 3-4

Super-Quick Chicken and Tomato

Tomato soup with basil and oregano makes a quick sauce for this chicken dish.

4	**boneless, skinless chicken breasts**	4
	oil spray for pan	
1	**tomato, sliced**	1
10 oz.	**can Campbell's tomato with basil and oregano soup or a similar product**	398 mL
	pepper to taste	

- Flatten chicken breasts in a small plastic bag or between 2 pieces of waxed paper with your hand or a meat mallet.

- Heat a large, non-stick cooking pan over medium-high heat and spray with vegetable oil. Add chicken breasts and cook for 2 minutes on each side.

- Top the chicken pieces with tomato slices and add the soup. Bring to a boil; reduce heat to simmer. Cover and cook for 8-10 minutes, until no pink color remains and juices run clear when the chicken is pierced with a small knife.

- Sprinkle with freshly ground pepper.

Serves 4

Chicken and Vegetable Stir-Fry

Bottled stir-fry sauce makes this a super-quick stir-fry.

1 tbsp.	vegetable oil	15 mL
4	boneless, skinless chicken breasts, cut into bite-sized pieces	4
4 cups	thinly sliced vegetables, such as celery, carrots, zucchini, broccoli, onion, tomato, cabbage	1 L
5 oz.	can sliced water chestnuts, drained (optional)	150 g
2 tbsp.	apple juice	30 mL
1/3 cup	bottled stir-fry sauce	75 mL

- Heat oil in a large, non-stick pan over medium-high heat. Add chicken pieces; stir and cook until the chicken is no longer pink, 4-5 minutes. Transfer chicken to a plate and cover.

- Increase heat slightly. Add vegetables. Stir and toss until tender-crisp, 2-3 minutes.

- Add chicken and juices, apple juice and stir-fry sauce. Cook and stir until heated through, 2-3 minutes. Serve with noodles or rice.

Serves 3-4

White Chili with Chicken

This chili is a welcome change from the tomato chili recipes.

2 tbsp.	vegetable oil	30 mL
3	boneless, skinless chicken breasts or 4 chicken thighs cut in 1/2" (1.3 cm) pieces	3
1	medium onion, peeled and chopped	1
1 tsp.	bottled minced garlic	5 mL
4 oz.	can diced green chilies	113 mL
1 tsp.	ground cumin	5 mL
1/4 tsp.	red pepper flakes	1 mL
2 x 14 oz.	cans white beans, drained and rinsed	2 x 398 g
2 cups	chicken stock OR water	500 mL
2 cups	grated mozzarella OR Monterey Jack cheese salt and pepper to taste	500 mL

- In a large non-stick saucepan, heat the oil over medium-high heat. Add the chicken and onion. Cook and stir until the onions are soft and the chicken almost cooked through, about 5 minutes

White Chili with Chicken *continued*

- Add the garlic, chilies, cumin, pepper flakes, beans and stock. Heat to boiling. Reduce heat to simmer and cook for 10 minutes.
- Serve in bowls and top with grated cheese.

Serves 4

Variation: Add sliced or grated carrots and celery with the onions.

Variation: Serve any leftovers on baked potatoes; top with grated cheese.

Tuscany Chicken and Tomatoes

Travel to Tuscany with this flavorful chicken dish. Serve with pasta (try penne, fusilli or linguine; cook according to package directions), chunks of fresh bread and a green salad.

1 lb.	or 6 pieces boneless, skinless chicken thighs	500 g
1 tsp.	Italian herb seasoning	5 mL
2 cups	frozen mixed vegetables (from a 1 lb. [500 g] package of international mix, including broccoli, cauliflower and carrots)	500 mL
2 x 14 oz.	can diced OR Italian-style tomatoes salt and pepper to taste	2 x 398 mL

- Trim fat from chicken thighs and cut into bite-sized pieces.
- Put chicken and remaining ingredients into a pot and bring to a boil. Stir; cover; reduce heat to a simmer. Cook for 10 minutes, stirring occasionally
- Season with salt and pepper. Serve with pasta or in bowls with toasted country-style bread.

Serves 4-6

Variation: For a more intense flavor, add ¹/₄-¹/₂ tsp. (1-2 mL) of dried hot pepper flakes and 2 cloves of chopped garlic when you combine the ingredients in the pot to cook.

Variation: If you have fresh vegetables on hand, you can use a variety of chopped vegetables, e.g., broccoli, cauliflower, carrots, red bell peppers, etc., or use only broccoli if you prefer. Mixed dried Italian herbs, about 1 tsp. (5 mL) add additional flavor.

TIP: Leftover cooked pasta can be stored, covered, in the fridge for a couple of days or in the freezer for weeks. To reheat, microwave for 3-4 minutes or dip into boiling water until heated through, about 3 minutes.

Chicken Pasta Sauce

This thick chunky family favorite uses prepared spaghetti sauce.

1 tbsp.	vegetable oil	15 mL
1 lb.	ground chicken OR turkey	500 g
14 oz.	can spaghetti sauce or 2 cups (500 mL) from a jar	398 mL
1 tsp.	EACH basil, oregano and sugar	5 mL
¼ tsp.	hot red pepper flakes	1 mL
	salt and pepper to taste	

- Heat oil in a large non-stick pan on medium-high. Add the chicken; cook and stir. Use a wooden spatula to break up the chicken as it cooks. Drain and blot with a paper towel to remove excess fat.

- Add spaghetti sauce, herbs, sugar and pepper flakes.

- Heat to boiling. Reduce heat; cover and simmer for 10 minutes, stirring often. Serve with your favorite pasta.

Serves 4

Variation: Use lean ground beef for **Beef Pasta Sauce**. Both sauces invite the addition of more vegetables; choose green and red peppers, onions, grated carrots and chunks of zucchini.

TIP: For 2 servings use only ½ lb. (250 g) ground chicken or beef. For 6 servings add a second can of spaghetti sauce.

Restaurants often cooked pasta in the refrigerator in cold water. Leftover pasta that you are keeping for the next day will taste fresher stored in this way. Don't store for longer than overnight.

Oven-Cooked Chicken Breasts

Quick and no mess. One day when I was particularly busy, I cooked chicken breasts like this in the oven. They were excellent, so I tried them with a variety of sauces. All were good. Sauce with your favorite homemade or purchased sauce, cook and slice the chicken breasts and they can top a salad or become part of a wrap or sandwich.

2	skinless, boneless chicken breasts	3
sprinkling	of seasoned salt and freshly ground pepper	sprinkling
	(Use Mrs. Dash and a little salt.)	

- Preheat oven to 425°F (220°C).

- Place chicken breasts in an ovenproof glass casserole. Sprinkle with seasonings; cover with a lid and cook for 15 minutes. To check for doneness – cut a small slit in the thickest part of 1 breast. Meat is cooked when no pink remains and juices are clear.

Variation: To sauce the chicken, use ¼ cup (60 mL) of your favorite barbecue, curry or stir-fry sauce or a commercial variety and cook as directed. A little hoisin sauce is also good.

TIP: It is important to use a glass oven dish.

TIP: For 4 breasts, use an oiled 1-1½-quart (1-1.5 L) casserole with a lid. Place breasts in a single layer. Sauce or season. Cover and cook for 10 minutes; change the positions of the breasts, inside edges to outside. Cook 5 minutes more and check for doneness. If the chicken is not quite cooked, return to oven for 2 or 3 minutes.

TIP: **Quick Defrosting**

- Store meats in 1-1½ lb. (500-750 g) amounts in the freezer. Leaving them in the store wrappings is fine.

- To defrost quickly when you are desperate for meat for dinner, run hot water over the package for about 30 seconds. Remove the plastic wrap, and pry off the bottom tray.

- Put the meat on a microwave-safe dish and microwave for 2-3 minutes on high. The meat will be thawed enough to transfer to a pan and begin browning. This works for ground meats, chicken breasts and thighs, chops and cuts up to ½" (1.3 cm) thick. This method thaws precooked meats and rice too.

TIP: When using the defrost cycle on the microwave, you will find newer microwaves, 1990 and newer, have efficient defrost cycles. They are programmed to defrost gently and are a true asset to quick cooks.

Turkey Italiano

The turkey takes only minutes to prepare, so have a salad or rice pilaf ready before you begin to cook.

1 tbsp.	vegetable oil	15 mL
1 lb.	uncooked boneless turkey breast slices or turkey cutlets	500 g
	salt and pepper to taste	
½ cup	prepared spaghetti sauce, chunky style	125 mL
6-8	thin mozzarella OR Monterey Jack cheese slices	6-8

- Heat oil in a large, non-stick pan over medium-high heat. Season the turkey slices with salt and pepper.

- Cook the turkey on both sides until it changes color and looks opaque, 2-3 minutes. Reduce heat to low.

- Spread spaghetti sauce on each turkey slice. Top with cheese. Cover with a lid until cheese is melted, about 2 minutes. Serve.

Serves 4

TIP: For tasty, tender turkey, chicken and pork, do not over cook. Cook just until the meat is heated through, with no pink color remaining. The meat will be juicy and tender.

Pictured on page 85.

Oven-Cooked Pork Chops

Quick and no mess. This recipe uses almost the same method as the chicken breasts on page 57. Use your favorite barbecue or stir-fry sauce or spray the chops with a little cooking oil and sprinkle with a commercial steak seasoning. Chops can be marinated in the sauce for ½ hour at room temperature or over night in the fridge, if you have time.

2	boneless pork loin chops, ¾" (2 cm) thick	2
	seasoning salt and pepper	
¼ cup	chicken broth or sauce of your choice	60 mL

Oven-Cooked Pork Chops *continued*

- Preheat oven to 450°F (230°C).

- Place pork chops in an ovenproof baking dish. Season; add salt and pepper; add broth or sauce. Cook for 10 minutes; turn chops over, baste and cook for 10 minutes more, or until done.

- To test, cut a small slit in the middle of one pork chop. The meat should be barely pink and still tender and juicy.

Serves 2

Beef Chili Pie

This is a favorite with kids and other hungry people. It's ready in 15 minutes.

4 cups	corn chips, coarsely crushed	1 L
1 lb.	lean ground beef	500 g
1	small onion, chopped	1
	a sprinkling of salt and pepper	
1 tsp.	chili powder	5 mL
14 oz.	can chili	398 mL
1 cup	shredded mozzarella cheese	250 mL

- Put the chips in a greased, microwave-safe, glass, 9" (23 cm) pie plate and set aside.

- In a large non-stick pan, cook meat and onion until no pink remains and the meat begins to brown. Break up meat with a fork or spatula as it cooks. Season with salt, pepper and chili powder.

- Drain the fat from the pan. Blot the meat with a paper towel to remove most of the remaining fat. Add canned chili and heat.

- Spoon meat mixture over the chips. Top with cheese and microwave on high until cheese begins to melt, 1-2 minutes. Serve with a crisp salad and garlic bread.

Serves 3-4

Variation: Serve with salsa and sour cream.

Variation: Add a can of corn niblets to the chili mixture.

Pizza Meat Loaf Pie

It takes longer to heat the oven than to prepare this meat loaf, so be sure to turn on the oven well in advance . . .

1 lb.	extra-lean ground beef	500 g
1	egg	1
1/4 cup	oatmeal	60 mL
1/4 cup	milk OR water	60 mL
1/2 tsp.	EACH salt and thyme	2 mL
1/4 tsp.	pepper	1 mL
1/4 cup	pizza sauce	60 mL
1 cup	grated pizza cheese	250 mL

- Preheat oven to 425°F (220°C). Spray a 9" (23 cm) pie plate with non-stick cooking spray.

- Mix beef, egg, oatmeal, milk, salt and pepper together. Press into the pie plate.

- Bake for 12-14 minutes. Drain off most of the accumulated liquid. Top the meat with the pizza sauce and cheese, and return to the oven until the sauce is hot and the cheese begins to melt, about 5 minutes.

Serves 4

Variation: Add 1/2 cup (125 mL) grated onions and carrots to the meat mixture and increase the initial baking time 3 minutes.

Ground Meat and Beans

Good, quick and satisfying. This dish is particularly satisfying when the kids make it for dinner and you go out! Serve with whole-wheat toast and carrot and celery sticks.

2 tbsp.	vegetable oil	30 mL
1/2-1 lb.	ground beef OR turkey	125-250 mL
1	small or medium onion, chopped	1
14 oz.	can baked beans (vegetarian OR pork and beans)	398 mL
2 tbsp.	ketchup	30 mL
1 tsp.	dry mustard	5 mL

Ground Meat and Beans *continued*

- In a large, non-stick pan, heat oil over medium-high heat. Add the meat and the onion. Cook until onion is soft and the meat has changed color and is cooked through.

- Add the beans, ketchup and mustard. Cook to heat through.

Serves 2-4

Chili or Salsa Hamburger Helper

This busy day standby is quick, filling and tasty, and much healthier and less expensive than the packaged version. Serve with a green salad and chunky bread.

1 tbsp.	vegetable oil	15 mL
1	medium onion, chopped	1
2	celery stalks, diced	2
1/2	red pepper, seeded and chopped	1/2
1 lb.	lean ground beef	500 g
28 oz.	can diced tomatoes	796 mL
1/4 cup	chili sauce OR salsa	60 mL
1 1/2 cups	small pasta such as broken noodles, fusilli or rotini	375 mL
	salt and pepper to taste	

- In a large, non-stick pan, heat oil over medium-high heat. Add onion, celery, red pepper and ground beef. Stir and cook until meat loses all trace of red and begins to brown. Drain off fat and blot the meat with a paper towel.

- Add tomatoes, chili sauce or salsa and pasta.

- Increase heat to bring mixture to a boil. Reduce heat and simmer until pasta is tender, about 10 minutes.

Variation: For faster preparation, use precooked ground meat. If you have precooked the pasta or you have some left over, it's an instant meal.

Variation: Add grated carrots and chopped zucchini or a 14 oz. (398 mL) can of chili-style red kidney beans.

SIDE DISHES

Salads, vegetables, rice, beans, breads

*M*any of the recipes in this book are for complete meals. When a side dish is needed, or when you want to complement the food being served, look here for super-quick suggestions from your cupboard and fridge.

Super-Quick Side Dishes

Following are quick dressups for salads, vegetables, rice, beans and breads.

Fruits and Vegetables

- sliced tomatoes or cucumbers
- carrot sticks and pepper strips
- canned baked beans
- bottled 3-bean salad
- fruit slices such as apples or pears
- canned or bottled applesauce
- canned pineapple rings or peach slices
- cantaloupe or honeydew melon slices
- washed ready-to-serve greens with sliced tomato or a peeled and sectioned orange

Deli Choices

- potato salad
- pasta salad
- 3-bean salad or coleslaw
- Greek salad
- fruit salad

Couscous, Instant Rice, Orzo and 5-Minute Potatoes

Use these quickly cooked favorites as a side dish, or in any pilaf or rice salad recipe. They become a main dish when you add stir-fried meat and vegetables. For more flavor, replace some of the water with chicken stock.

Couscous
For 3 cups (750 mL) of couscous, bring 1 1/2 cups (375 mL) of water to a boil, add 1 cup (250 mL) of couscous and 1/4 tsp. (1 mL) salt. Cover and remove from heat. Let stand for 5 minutes. Fluff with a fork and serve.

Instant Rice
Microwave: For 3 cups (750 mL) of instant rice, combine 1 1/2 cups (375 mL) of water with 1 1/2 cups (375 mL) of instant rice and 1/2 tsp. (2 mL) salt in a microwaveable casserole. Microwave on high until the mixture boils, 3-5 minutes. Remove from oven. Let stand 5 minutes. Fluff with a fork and serve. **Stove top method:** In a pot over high heat, bring rice, water and salt to a boil. Remove pot from heat, cover and let stand for 5 minutes. Fluff with a fork and serve.

Quick Pilafs
You can use instant rice, leftover rice or precooked frozen rice. To thaw, place the rice in a microwave-safe container and heat on high for 1 minute per cup (250 mL) of rice. **To the rice add:**

- A few raisins, chopped pecans and a pinch of cloves, heat for 3 minutes on high.
- 1 cup (250 mL) of frozen sweetlet peas, heat for 3 minutes on high.
- In a non-stick pan over medium-high heat, cook a little chopped onion, celery, a few chopped mushrooms and 1/4 cup (60 mL) slivered almonds for 2 or 3 minutes. Add 1 tbsp. (15 mL) soy sauce to the pan. Finally, add 2 cups (500 mL) thawed, cooked rice. Toss and stir for a few minutes, until heated through.

Orzo or Small Shell Pasta
Bring 3 cups (750 mL) of water to a boil, add 1 cup (250 mL) of orzo or small shell pasta and 1/2 tsp. (2 mL) of salt. Reduce the heat and cook for 10-12 minutes, until pasta is tender but still firm. Rinse and drain.

5-Minute Potatoes
Put 2 or 3 peeled and sliced potatoes in a microwaveable casserole, sprinkle with 1 tbsp. (15 mL) of water, seasoning salt and freshly ground black pepper. Microwave on high for 5 minutes. For 5 potatoes, increase microwave time to 10-12 minutes.

Salad Greens

The supermarket and our gardens offer a wide choice of greens. We can easily find romaine, red and green leaf lettuce and iceberg. Vary your choices to include taste, texture and color. Be sure to include baby spinach and young beet greens from the garden. For instant salad dressing, drizzle greens with extra-virgin olive oil, a little red wine or cider vinegar, a little sugar, salt and pepper (about ¹/₂ tsp. [2 mL] each) and a sprinkle of bottled salad seasoning. Toss and serve. Or add a basic vinaigrette.

Here are a few combos to add to your bed of greens:

- 1 large tomato, chopped; 2-3 tbsp. (30-45 mL) of chopped red onion; and ¹/₄ cup (60 mL) crumbled feta cheese. Add ¹/₂ tsp. (2 mL) dried basil or a few leaves of fresh.

- 1-2 cups (250-500 mL) baby spinach leaves; ¹/₄ cup (60 mL) chopped red onion; a peeled and chopped orange or 1 cup (250 mL) halved strawberries. Add ¹/₄ cup (60 mL) toasted almonds.

- 2 Portobello mushrooms, sliced and sautéed in 1 tbsp. (15 mL) butter or olive oil until tender and browned a little. Sprinkle with balsamic vinegar; add to the greens and top with toasted, slivered almonds.

- ¹/₂ cup (125 mL) frozen corn kernels (rinse with hot water to thaw); 1 red pepper, seeded and chopped, and 4 green onions, sliced, using some of the tops.

- Chopped broccoli and cauliflower, red onion and real bacon bits.

- ¹/₂ peeled, seeded cucumber, chopped; 4 oz. (113 g) can shrimp, rinsed and drained.

- ¹/₄ cup (60 mL) sliced black olives, halved cherry tomatoes, a little chopped red onion, cucumber and crumbled feta cheese.

- Leftover corn salad or bean salad.

TIP: Vegetable oil, canola, safflower, soybean, corn oil and vegetable oil blends all have fairly bland flavors and are interchangeable for salads.

TIP: Olive oil has a very distinctive flavor – when a recipe specifies olive oil, it will give you the best flavor.

TIP: Use red wine vinegar, rice wine vinegar or balsamic as directed – they each have distinctive flavors.

Try some of these already-prepared additions, singly or in combination:

- Sliced, pre-washed baby carrots.

- Cabbage or broccoli coleslaw mixes.

- Chopped, prepared stir-fry veggies.

- Canned 3-bean salad, rinsed and drained, or drained kernel corn.

- Orange or grapefruit segments.

- Apple slices dipped in lemon juice.

- Bottled sun-dried tomatoes, roasted red peppers and artichoke hearts, drained and chopped.

- Frozen kernel corn or tiny sweet peas, to thaw place in a strainer and run a little warm water over them.

- Yesterday's leftover veggies.

- Croûtons or toasted sunflower seeds or slivered almonds.

Preparing Salad Greens

Many people don't make salads because they don't like washing and preparing the greens. To relieve the tedium, try this: fill the kitchen sink with cold water. Cut off the base of the heads of 1 romaine and 1 leaf lettuce. Put the leaves in the water; remove 2 or 3 at a time, lifting from the stem end. Swish leaves a little, to remove the sand and grit. Drain in a colander and spin in a salad spinner or spread out on a tea towel, cover with a second towel, roll gently, unroll, move the leaves around and roll again. Remove the leaves from the towels or spinner.

Store in a zip-lock bag in the fridge. Placing a paper towel in the bag absorbs extra moisture and helps to keep the greens fresh and crisp. A head of romaine and 1 of leaf lettuce is a lot of washing and wrapping, but worth the effort as you will have salad greens for many days ahead.

Look for the display of prepared salads and greens in the produce department and choose one of the many prepared products, mixed greens, broccoli and cabbage slaws, salads complete with dressings and croûtons. They may seem expensive but there is no waste and they're saving you time. They're also saving you money and adding nutrition, if the alternative is a fast food pizza or burger.

Salad Dressings

These homemade salad dressings are fresh tasting, economical and low in fat. Make your favorite and store it in the fridge.

Simple Vinaigrette

This quick dressing doubles as a marinade or a sauce for basting grilled meats or vegetables.

$\frac{1}{2}$ cup	olive OR vegetable oil	125 mL
2 tbsp.	cider vinegar	30 mL
2 tsp.	creamy Dijon mustard blend	10 mL
	salt and freshly ground pepper to taste	

• Combine all the ingredients in a jar and shake to blend. Add salt and pepper to taste.

Makes $\frac{2}{3}$ cup (150 mL)

Thai Salad Dressing

Use this low-fat dressing with field greens or mixed greens topped with sliced grilled chicken. It also complements a spinach, orange and almond salad or a strawberry, pecan and romaine combination.

2 tbsp.	soy sauce	30 mL
$\frac{1}{4}$ cup	cider vinegar	60 mL
1 tbsp.	brown sugar	15 mL
1 tsp.	ground ginger	5 mL
2 tsp.	Dijon mustard	10 mL
$\frac{1}{4}$ cup	salad oil	60 mL
2 tsp.	sesame oil	10 mL
$\frac{1}{4}$ cup	water	60 mL

• Whisk all ingredients in a small bowl or jar. Store unused dressing in the fridge.

Makes about $1\frac{1}{2}$ cups (375 mL)

Yogurt Dill Dressing

Good with tomato cucumber salad, potato salad and as a vegetable dip.

1/4 cup	yogurt	60 mL
1/4 cup	mayonnaise	60 mL
2 tsp.	sugar OR liquid honey	10 mL
1 tbsp.	cider vinegar	15 mL
1 tsp.	dried dillweed	5 mL
	salt and pepper to taste	

• Combine all ingredients. Serve as a salad dressing or dip.

Makes 1/2 cup (125 mL)

Creamy Low-Fat Dressing

This fresh tasting dressing invites the addition of chopped cucumber or crumbled blue cheese. Serve it with romaine and a few slices of tomato and cucumber.

1/2 cup	light mayonnaise	125 mL
1/2 cup	skim-milk yogurt	125 mL
2 tbsp.	vinegar of choice, I like cider or rice vinegar	30 mL
1/2 tsp.	bottled minced garlic	2 mL
1/2 tsp.	dried dillweed	2 mL
1/2 tsp.	salt	2 mL
	freshly ground black pepper	

• In a small bowl, whisk all ingredients until blended. Serve. Store unused dressing in the fridge.

Makes 1 cup (250 mL)

Variation: For a **Chunky Dressing**, add 1/2 cup (125 mL) seeded, peeled and chopped cucumber, with or without the dried dillweed.

Variation: For **Blue Cheese Dressing**, omit the dried dillweed and add 2 tbsp. (30 mL) or more of crumbled blue cheese.

TIP: This dressing makes a good dip for veggies and a super topping for baked potatoes.

Salad Every Day

When you are longing for some fresh flavors, top your bowl of mixed greens with one of the following combos and toss with your choice of dressing.

Apples and Pecans

- 2 Granny Smith apples, quartered, cored and thinly sliced and ¹/₂ cup (125 mL) toasted pecan halves

Pears and Grapes

- 2 ripe pears, quartered, sliced and dipped in lemon juice, with 1 cup (250 mL) of green or black grapes, halved and seeded, and crumbled blue cheese (optional)

Cucumber and Apple with Raisins and Nuts

- 1 medium-sized cucumber, peeled, seeded and coarsely chopped, and 1 Granny Smith apple, cored and diced. Add a few golden raisins and ¹/₂ cup (125 mL) walnut pieces

Variations: *Crumbled or grated tofu can be added to these salads. Crumbled feta cheese is good too.*

SUMMER TOMATOES

Fresh tomatoes from the vine mean we can eat our fill. Slice and serve fresh tomatoes or try one of these easy ways to prepare them.

Marinated Tomatoes

4	large tomatoes, sliced	4
2 tsp.	sugar	10 mL
2 tbsp.	vinegar	30 mL
¹/₂ cup	fresh basil leaves or a sprinkling of dried basil	125 mL
	salt and pepper to taste	

- Slice the tomatoes and arrange in a shallow dish or plate. Tuck basil leaves under and around tomato slices.

- Sprinkle with sugar, vinegar, salt and pepper. Cover with plastic wrap until ready to serve. Serve at room temperature.

Variation: Add a sprinkling of oregano and some crumbled feta cheese.

Tomatoes, Mozzarella and Basil

3-4	large ripe tomatoes, 8-12 slices	3-4
8-12	slices mozzarella cheese	8-12
2-4 tbsp.	olive oil	30-60 mL
16	basil leaves or 1 tsp. (5 mL) dried	16
	freshly ground pepper to taste	

• Arrange cheese and tomato slices alternately on a serving plate or 4 individual salad plates. Chop basil leaves and sprinkle over the tomato and cheese. Drizzle with oil and add a grinding of pepper.

Serves 4

Variation: Add some black Greek olives or spiced olives.

Pictured on page 35.

Creamy Cucumber and Lime Salad

The summer the garden produced tons of cucumbers I developed this cucumber topping for greens. For a side dish, increase the amount of cucumber and serve with fish, grilled chicken, hamburgers and curries.

2 cups	peeled, seeded, finely chopped cucumber	500 mL
3/4 cup	plain non-fat yogurt	175 mL
2 tsp.	sugar	10 mL
1	green onion, chopped (use most of the greens)	1
1	lime, 1 tbsp. (15 mL) of juice and about 1/2 tsp. (2 mL) of grated peel	1
1 1/2 tsp.	chopped fresh dillweed (optional) salt and pepper	7 mL

• Mix all of the ingredients together. Serve on salad greens.

Serves 4-6

When the kids are whining and clamoring for supper, put out veggies and dip for them to snack on while the meal is being prepared. A quick dip that kids like is 1/2 cup (125 mL) yogurt with 2 tbsp. (30 mL) of cucumber salad dressing.

Spinach and Apple Salad

This fresh-tasting salad is loaded with goodness.

1	Granny Smith apple, thinly sliced	1
1 tbsp.	lemon juice for dipping apple slices	15 mL
10 oz.	pkg. fresh spinach, washed and stemmed, use as much as needed	283 g
½ cup	diced Gouda cheese	125 mL
½ cup	coarsely chopped pecans	125 mL

Dressing

2 tsp.	olive oil	10 mL
4 tbsp.	cider vinegar	60 mL
2 tbsp.	brown sugar	30 mL

- Coat apple slices with lemon juice.

- Tear large spinach leaves into smaller pieces. Toss spinach and apple slices in a large bowl. Add cheese and pecans.

- Combine dressing ingredients. Add to salad; toss and serve.

4 servings

Variation: Use the same salad dressing but add 1 cup (250 mL) of sliced strawberries and 1 cup (250 mL) of sliced mushrooms to the spinach. Omit the cheese and pecans.

Cabbage Coleslaw

Here are 2 cabbage salads that invite variations. They are good keepers, too, and with the addition of another vegetable, sunflower seeds or nuts, they can be served again. Buy a prepared coleslaw mix or use your processor to grate the cabbage and carrot.

3 cups	shredded green cabbage	750 mL
1	large carrot, grated	1
1	green apple, chopped	1
2 tbsp.	bacon bits (optional)	30 mL

Creamy Mustard Dressing

⅓ cup	light mayonnaise	75 mL
⅓ cup	plain yogurt	75 mL
2 tbsp.	cider vinegar	30 mL
1 tbsp.	sugar	15 mL
½ tsp.	dry mustard	2 mL
	salt and pepper	

Cabbage Coleslaw *continued*

- Combine the cabbage, carrot, green apple and bacon bits in a bowl.
- Mix dressing ingredients; add to salad. Toss. Serve or refrigerate, covered.

Variations: Add 1 cup (250 mL) of finely chopped celery.

- Add $\frac{1}{2}$ cup (125 mL) of washed raisins and $\frac{1}{2}$ cup (125 mL) chopped walnuts or pecans.
- In place of the apple, add 1 cup (250 mL) of green grapes, halved, and 1 cup (250 mL) of drained pineapple tidbits.
- Sunflower seeds are good too.
- Replace some of the cabbage with broccoli slaw mix.
- Leftover coleslaw with deli meats and cheese is good in buns and wraps.

TIP: For a milder flavor, use 1 tbsp. (15 mL) vinegar; $\frac{1}{4}$ tsp. (1 mL) dry mustard.

TIP: Peeled broccoli stems can be chopped in a food processor or grated and added to salads.

Crunchy Sweet and Sour Slaw

This recipe has swept the nation, make it often. The leftovers are good too.

3 oz.	pkg. Oriental OR chicken-flavored ramen (Japanese noodle) soup mix	85 g
3 tbsp.	soy sauce	45 mL
2 tbsp.	vinegar	30 mL
1 tbsp.	sugar	15 mL
$\frac{1}{4}$ cup	vegetable oil	60 mL
2 cups	prepackaged coleslaw mix	500 mL
2 cups	broccoli slaw mix	500 mL
$\frac{1}{2}$ cup	EACH toasted sliced almonds, and unsalted sunflower seeds	125 mL
	sprinkling of freshly ground pepper	

- In a large serving bowl, Combine the noodle flavor packet mix with soy sauce, vinegar, sugar and oil. Beat with a whisk or fork to blend.
- Chop the coleslaw and broccoli slaw mixes a little and break up the noodles. Add to the dressing.
- Toss well. Garnish with the nuts and seeds.

Serves 4-6

Variation: Add grated carrot, chopped green, red or yellow peppers, Chinese cabbage, celery or bean sprouts.

TIP: To make ahead, combine dressing and vegetables and store in fridge in a covered container. Add nuts and noodles at the last minute – to keep crunchy.

Mixed Bean Salad

This salad will keep, covered, in the fridge for several days. Serve as a side dish or on a bed of greens.

19 oz.	can black OR cannellini* beans, rinsed and drained or a mixture of beans of your choice	**540 mL**
14 oz.	can kernel corn, drained	**398 mL**
2	celery stalks, diced	**2**
½ cup	chunky medium salsa	**125 mL**
¼ cup	cider vinegar (white can be used)	**60 mL**
¼ cup	vegetable oil	**60 mL**
¼ cup	sugar	**60 mL**
	salt and pepper to taste	

- Mix all the ingredients in a bowl. Serve at once, or cover and store in the fridge until needed.

Serves 4

* Large, white Italian kidney beans

Variation: Add 1-2 cups (250-500 mL) chopped tomatoes or halved cherry tomatoes, ½ cup (125 mL) chopped red or green onions and ½ cup (125 mL) chopped celery, if you choose.

Pictured on page 35.

Calico Corn

A make-ahead, keep-in-the-fridge side dish.

14 oz.	can corn niblets	**398 mL**
1 cup	frozen small green peas	**250 mL**
1	small red onion, finely chopped	**1**
1	green pepper, seeded and chopped	**1**
¼ cup	bottled Italian OR French dressing	**60 mL**

- Combine veggies in a bowl. Serve or store, covered, in the fridge.

Variation: For a salad with a southwest flavor, omit the bottled dressing and add a 14 oz. (398 mL) can of diced plum Italian tomatoes, drained, and a 14 oz. (398 mL) can of kidney beans, drained. Add the following dressing.

Calico Corn *continued*

Southwest Dressing

2 tbsp.	cider OR white vinegar	30 mL
2 tbsp.	vegetable oil	30 mL
1 tsp.	chili powder	5 mL
¼ tsp.	red pepper flakes	1 mL
½ tsp.	cumin	2 mL

Combine all ingredients and add to Calico Corn salad.

Potato and Vegetable Salad with Dill

This recipe keeps well in the fridge; expand with vegetables of your choice.

1½ lbs.	red OR Yukon Gold potatoes, washed and cut into 1" (2.5 cm) pieces	750 g
1 tsp.	salt	5 mL
	sprinkling of black pepper	
1 tbsp.	cider vinegar	15 mL
¼ cup	non-fat yogurt	60 mL
¼ cup	mayonnaise	60 mL
2 tsp.	Dijon mustard	10 mL
1	celery stalk, chopped	1
¼ cup	chopped green or red onion	60 mL
1	medium carrot, washed and grated on medium holes of grater	1
1 tbsp.	chopped fresh dillweed or 1 tsp. (5 mL) dried	15 mL

- Cook potatoes in a large saucepan with 1 tsp. (5 mL) salt until tender, about 9 minutes. Drain and transfer to a plate, spread out a little so that they will cool. Sprinkle with pepper.

- In a large bowl, whisk together vinegar, yogurt, mayonnaise, mustard, celery, onion, carrot and dillweed.

- Add potatoes. Toss and mix gently until combined. Serve or cover and store in the fridge.

Serves 4

Variation: Include your favorite vegetables; try chopped cucumbers, tiny peas, green beans, chopped sweet red and green peppers.

TIP: New potatoes, and especially Yukon Gold, do not need to be peeled. Wash well and cut into pieces.

Wild Rice and Fruit Salad

For a quick version of this dish use leftover cooked rice – white, brown or wild. For the wild rice goodness in a hurry, use the prepackaged long-grain and wild rice mix. I like it best with wild rice and I use precooked rice that I have stored in the freezer.

3 cups	cold, cooked rice OR 6 oz. (180 g) pkg. of long-grain and wild rice mix, cooked, discard flavor packet	750 mL
1 cup	low-fat or skim-milk yogurt	250 mL
1 tbsp.	fresh lemon juice	15 mL
1 tbsp.	brown sugar OR honey	15 mL
¼ tsp.	EACH dried ginger and cloves	1 mL
1	orange, peeled and segmented, or about 1 cup (250 mL) canned apricots, quartered	1
¼ cup	raisins, washed	60 mL
2 cups	halved strawberries OR halved black grapes OR sliced kiwi OR a combination	500 mL
½ cup	slivered almonds, OR sunflower seeds, toasted, use either or a combination	125 mL
	salt and pepper to taste	

- Prepare the rice.

- In a large bowl, combine the yogurt, lemon juice, sugar, ginger and cloves. Add oranges, raisins, and fruit. Add the rice. Stir and toss. Add the nuts just before serving.

- Serve salad at once or store, covered, in the fridge until needed.

Serves 4-6

Variation: For a vegetable version, use chopped broccoli, cauliflower, sliced strawberries and oranges and ¼ cup (60 mL) of real bacon pieces, 2-3 cups (500-750 mL) of vegetables and fruit in all.

Variation: Make this salad with wild or brown rice or combine wild or brown rice with long-grain white rice.

VEGETABLES

Quick Dress-Ups for Vegetables

- Add a sprinkle of lemon juice and toasted, slivered almonds to cooked broccoli or green beans.

- Sprinkle shredded Cheddar or mozzarella cheese on cooked broccoli or cabbage, or lay 2 slices of cheese on the vegetables and microwave for 1 minute to melt.

- Toss tender-crisp cooked vegetables with 1 tbsp. (15 mL) butter (or butter seasoning), salt and pepper and a squeeze of lemon juice.

- Combine sour cream, yogurt and a dash of lime juice with sliced cucumbers.

- Basil or Italian seasoning perks up cooked green beans, as does garlic salt and lemon juice.

- Toss cooked green beans or broccoli with bacon bits.

- Cooked potatoes and potato salad like parsley and dillweed.

- For cooked carrots, add a little orange juice or a little nutmeg and brown sugar.

- When serving a plate of fresh vegetables try this dip: mix 1 cup (250 mL) of sour cream or yogurt with a little salt and pepper, 1 tsp. (5 mL) lemon juice, 1 tsp. (5 mL) of dried dillweed or salad seasoning and $\frac{1}{2}$ tsp. (2 mL) of sugar.

Eat your vegetables! It's a pleasure! Vegetables are best eaten in season as is, simply prepared or with dips. They can be served as snacks, side dishes or as a saucy main dish. When you cook them, enhance their flavor with a little lemon or lime juice, a little sugar, honey or vinegar or with butter or margarine and salt and pepper.

Baked Tomato Halves

Quickly prepared, baked in a toaster oven or as part of an oven meal, these tomatoes are ready in minutes.

2-3	large tomatoes, cut in half	2-3
1/2 cup	fine dried bread crumbs	125 mL
1 tbsp.	olive oil OR butter	15 mL
1/2 tsp.	EACH dried oregano and basil	2 mL
	salt and pepper to taste	

- Heat toaster oven (or oven) to 400°F (200°C).

- Cut tomatoes in half. Scoop out a little pulp and seeds and place tomato halves on a pan.

- Mix crumbs, oil or butter and herbs. Spread the crumbs on the tomato halves; bake until heated through and the crumbs are lightly browned, 10-12 minutes.

Serves 4

TIP: As part of an oven meal, cook tomatoes for 12-15 minutes at 350°F (180°C).

Baked Stuffed Mushrooms

8	very large mushroom caps	8
1/4 cup	fine dry bread crumbs	60 mL
1 tbsp.	butter	15 mL
1/4 cup	freshly grated Parmesan cheese	60 mL
1	garlic clove, minced or 1/2 tsp. (2 mL) minced bottled garlic	1
	salt and pepper to taste	

- Heat toaster oven or oven to 400°F (200°C).

- Cut out the stem and a little of the center of the mushroom.

- Mix crumbs, butter, cheese, garlic, salt and pepper.

- Spoon the crumbs into the mushroom caps. Bake until heated through and the crumbs are lightly browned, 10-12 minutes.

Serves 4

TIP: The tomatoes and mushrooms are at their best when served within a few minutes of cooking.

Green Beans

Here are 2 ways to perk up your green beans . . .

4 cups	frozen green beans or garden beans, trimmed and halved	1 L
¼-½ tsp.	garlic salt	1-2 mL
½	lemon, juice of	½
	sprinkle of pepper	

- Cook frozen or fresh green beans in 1″ (2.5 cm) of boiling water, covered, until tender-crisp, 3-4 minutes. Drain.

- Sprinkle with garlic salt, lemon juice and pepper. Stir and serve.

Serves 4

Variation: Sauté 8 ozs. (250 g) of sliced mushrooms and 1 tsp. (5 mL) of minced onion until soft, 3-5 minutes. Toss with the cooked beans and sprinkle with salt and pepper.

Broccoli

Broccoli again? Yes, because it tastes good; it's a cancer fighter and a very good source of fiber. Here are some flavor perks to try.

4 cups	washed, peeled, bite-sized broccoli pieces	1 L

- Cook broccoli in 1″ (2.5 cm) of boiling water in a covered pot until tender-crisp, about 2 minutes. Drain.
- **Turn broccoli into a bowl and top with ONE of the following**:
  - ½ cup (125 mL) crumbled feta cheese
  - ¾ cup (175 mL) grated Cheddar cheese
  - a sprinkling of lemon juice, salt and pepper
  - 1 tbsp. (15 mL) melted butter
  - 1 tbsp. (15 mL) vinegar, try balsamic
  - a sprinkling of salt, pepper and sugar
  - toasted, slivered almonds and grated Parmesan cheese

Serves 4

Zucchini de la Maison

This dish, with its wonderful aroma, needs only a stir or 2 while you are prepar-ing the main dish. It tastes as good as it looks.

1	EACH yellow and green zucchini, use 2 green	1
	if you can't get yellow (2-3 cups [500-750 mL]	
	of sliced)	
2 tbsp.	butter (for flavor)	30 mL
2	garlic cloves, crushed	2
2 cups	cherry tomatoes	500 mL

- Cut the zucchini in half lengthwise and then into ½" (1.3 cm) slices.

- Heat the butter in a large non-stick pan over medium heat. Add the garlic and the zucchini.

- Cook and turn until heated through and beginning to brown.

- Add the tomatoes and cook until the tomatoes are heated through but not bursting. Serve immediately.

Serves 4

Pictured on page 85.

Carrots with Orange Glaze

This is the way my mother cooked carrots when I was a child. I loved them.

3-4	carrots, grated on a medium-size grater	3-4
¼ cup	orange juice OR 1 tbsp. (15 mL) frozen orange juice concentrate and ¼ cup (60 mL) of water	60 mL
1 tbsp.	butter	15 mL
	salt and pepper to taste	
sprinkle	sugar	sprinkle

- Combine all of the ingredients in a saucepan.

- Heat on medium high and bring to a boil. Cover and reduce heat; steam for 3 minutes. Stir once during cooking. Carrots should be tender-crisp.

Serves 4

Carrots and Green Grapes

3-4 cups	sliced carrots	750 mL-1 L
1 cup	green seedless grapes, halved	250 mL
	salt and pepper to taste	

- Cover the carrots with water and cook until tender-crisp, about 5 minutes. Drain.

- Add the grapes. Heat and stir for 1-2 minutes, just until the grapes are warm. Season with salt and pepper and serve.

Serves 4

TIP: For convenience use ready-to-eat peeled carrots, cut in half lengthwise.

Buy large bags of frozen vegetables and fruits, use what you need and re-seal. Store the remainder in the freezer.

RICE

*B*y itself or combined with other ingredients rice is a side dish. When you add meat or eggs and serve it with a salad, it is a meal. Rice stores well, is nutritious and easy to prepare.

There are many kinds of rice and rice products. Read the labels to become familiar with them and with the cooking directions. For most recipes I use long-grain white rice. One cup (250 mL) of rice and 2 cups (500 mL) of water makes 3 cups (750 mL) of rice in about 18 minutes. I appreciate the rice cooker, especially when I am trying to do 5 things at once. It cooks the rice automatically with perfect results every time. Brown rice and wild rice take longer to cook but they have more flavor and fiber than white and are often combined with white rice in pilafs and casseroles. Basmati rice has a lovely nutty flavor and cooks in 15 minutes.

Cooked rice stores well in the fridge for a few days and in the freezer for months. I cook double and triple quantities of rice and store the extra in 3-cup (750 mL) batches in the freezer.

TIP: To reheat rice, put 3 tbsp. (45 mL) of water in a pot. Add the rice (thawed, if frozen) and simmer 5-10 minutes. In the microwave, heat frozen rice in a covered casserole on high for about 1 minute per cup (250 mL).

Plain Boiled Rice with a Difference

Follow the package directions for cooking 1 cup (250 mL) of rice and add 1 of the following combinations:

- ¼ tsp. (1 mL) of saffron threads to the cooking water.

- chopped green and red pepper at the end of the cooking time – or 4 or 5 chopped green onions.

- 1 cup (250 mL) of frozen tiny peas. Stir in; cover the pot and put it back on the element for a few minutes.

- ¼ cup (60 mL) EACH of grated carrot, toasted sliced almonds and raisins.

- ¼ cup (60 mL) of chicken broth, ¼ tsp. (1 mL) EACH of cinnamon, cloves and cardamom, and 1 cup (250 mL) of washed sultana raisins or halved seedless green grapes

Fried Rice

Fried rice is always made with pre-cooked rice. It is quick to cook and can be a side dish or a full meal.

1 tbsp.	vegetable oil OR peanut oil	15 mL
2	green onions, chopped	2
2	eggs, beaten (use a cup and fork)	2
3 cups	cooked rice	750 mL
	salt and pepper	
	soy sauce	

- In a large non-stick pan, heat the oil over medium-high heat.

- Add the onion; fry and stir for about 30 seconds.

- Add the egg. Tip the pan to spread the egg. Stir to break it up and cook until beginning to set.

- Add the rice. Cook and stir until heated through, about 4 minutes. Add salt and pepper. Serve and pass the soy sauce.

Variations are Endless: Add about ½ cup (125 mL) thawed frozen peas, cut up green beans or broccoli, finely chopped cooked chicken or pork, or a few shrimp. Top with chopped bacon or peanuts, a drizzle of sesame oil is good, too.

Mexican Rice

A flavorful rice to serve with grilled meat or chicken, when you add leftover chicken or pork it can be a one-dish meal.

1 tbsp.	olive oil OR vegetable oil	15 mL
1/3 cup	finely chopped onion	75 mL
2	garlic cloves, finely chopped or 1 tsp. (5 mL) bottled minced garlic	2
1/4 tsp.	dried oregano	1 mL
1/4 tsp.	ground cumin	1 mL
1 tsp.	salt	5 mL
1 cup	long-grain white rice	250 mL
1	small zucchini, diced	1
1 cup	corn niblets (frozen)	250 mL
14 oz.	can stewed tomatoes (Mexican-style if available)	398 mL
2 cups	broth OR water	500 mL

- In a large saucepan, heat oil over medium-high heat. Add onion and cook until soft, about 3 minutes. Reduce heat to medium; add garlic, oregano, cumin and salt. Cook and stir for 1 minute.

- Add rice, zucchini and corn. Add tomatoes and broth; stir and bring the mixture to a boil. Reduce heat to low; cover and simmer for 20 minutes, or until rice is tender.

Serves 4

Caribbean Rice and Red Beans

Red beans and rice with the tropical taste of the Caribbean.

1 tbsp.	vegetable oil	15 mL
1	onion, chopped	1
1 cup	long-grain rice	250 mL
1 tsp.	EACH chili powder, cumin, salt	5 mL
2 cups	boiling water	500 mL
14 oz.	can red kidney beans, rinsed and drained	398 mL
1	green pepper, seeded and chopped	1

Caribbean Rice and Red Beans *continued*

- In a medium-sized pot or Dutch oven, heat oil over medium-high heat. Add onion and cook until soft and lightly browned on the edges, about 5 minutes.

- Add the rice and stir until coated.

- Add chili powder, cumin and salt. Stir. Cook about 1 minute. (Heating the spices releases their flavors.)

- Add water and bring to a boil. Stir. Reduce heat and simmer about 20 minutes. Rice will be nearly done.

- Add the rinsed beans and the green pepper. Stir gently. Cook for about 5 minutes, until beans are heated through.

Serves 4-6

Variation: This is a very adaptable dish. Add 2 crushed garlic cloves with the onions and/or a 14 oz. (398 mL) can of diced tomatoes with the beans. You may like to add ¼ tsp. (1 mL) of dried red pepper flakes too.

TIP: To save a few minutes, try preheating the beans in the microwave on high for 5 minutes.

Rice Pilaf with Cashews

Try this. Cooking the cashews gives them a less crunchy texture.

1 tbsp.	vegetable oil OR butter OR margarine	15 mL
½ cup	EACH finely chopped onion and celery	125 mL
1 cup	rice	250 mL
2 cups	chicken broth	500 mL
1 cup	raw cashews	250 mL
1 tsp.	salt	5 mL
¼ tsp.	cumin	1 mL

- In a large pot, heat the oil on high. Add onions and celery. Reduce heat a little; cook and stir until soft, about 3 minutes.

- Add rice and stir; add broth, salt, cashews and cumin.

- Bring to a boil. Reduce heat and simmer for 15-20 minutes, until the liquid is absorbed and the rice is cooked.

Variation: Omit the cumin and add 1 tsp. (5 mL) dried coriander or ¼ cup (60 mL) chopped fresh coriander (cilantro).

Pilaf with Saffron and Raisins

Saffron and cardamom contribute the color and aroma to this dish. If you don't have them add ¹/₈ tsp. (0.5 mL) of cloves. For a quick version, using pre-cooked rice, see method 2 below.

1 tsp.	vegetable oil	5 mL
1	onion, finely chopped	1
1 cup	rice	250 mL
2¹/₄ cups	water	550 mL
¹/₂ tsp.	grated lime zest	2 mL
¹/₄ tsp.	saffron threads	1 mL
1 tbsp.	lime juice	15 mL
¹/₄ tsp.	cinnamon	1 mL
¹/₄ tsp.	red pepper flakes	1 mL
¹/₈ tsp.	cardamom	0.5 mL
¹/₄ cup	bleached sultana raisins	1 mL

- In a medium-sized non-stick saucepan, heat the oil on medium-high. Add the onion. Stir and cook for 1-2 minutes. Add the rice and stir. Cook until the onion is soft and the rice coated with oil, 2-3 minutes.

- Add the water or broth and the remaining ingredients, except the raisins. Bring to a boil; reduce to a simmer. Cook for 15 minutes, or until done.

- Remove from the heat and stir in raisins. Let sit for 5 minutes and serve.

Serves 4

Variation: Add ¹/₂ cup (125 mL) toasted, slivered almonds with the raisins.

Method 2: Using Pre-Cooked Rice

- Heat 1 tsp. (5 mL) vegetable oil in a non-stick pan over medium-high heat. Add onion and cook until the onion is soft, 2-3 minutes. Remove from heat and add ¹/₄ cup (60 mL) water or chicken broth, lime zest, saffron, cinnamon, red pepper flakes, cardamom and raisins. Gently stir spice mixture into reheated rice.

- Or, put rice and spice mixture in a casserole and heat in the microwave on high for 2-3 minutes. Serve.

Pictured on the opposite page.

A QUICK AND EASY DINNER MENU

Turkey Italiano, page 58

Zucchini de la Maison, page 78

Pilaf with Saffron and Raisins, page 84

Wild Rice and Veggies

Try this with grilled steak or chicken. This dish travels well too. Take it to a potluck.

6½ oz.	pkg. long grain wild rice mix	180 g
1 tbsp.	vegetable oil	15 mL
1 cup	sliced mushrooms	250 mL
½	red bell pepper, chopped	½
4	green onions, chopped (use most of the greens)	4
½ cup	slivered almonds	125 mL
1 tsp.	bottled, minced ginger or grated fresh	5 mL
2 tbsp.	soy sauce	30 mL
	freshly grated pepper	

- Prepare wild rice according to package directions; discard flavor packet.

- Meanwhile, in a large, non-stick pan, heat oil over medium-high heat. Add mushrooms, pepper, onions and almonds. Cook and stir for about 2 minutes. Add ginger and continue to cook until the veggies are soft and beginning to brown, 3-4 minutes.

- Stir in soy sauce and pepper.

- Combine rice mixture and vegetables and serve.

Serves 4-6

Variation: Add 8 oz. (250 g) of chicken or beef strips when cooking the vegetable mixture. Cook for an additional 4-5 minutes.

Variation: The choice of vegetables depends on what you have on hand or what you prefer. Try sliced celery, broccoli stems, chopped carrots, peas, green beans and/or chopped water chestnuts.

TIP: Leftovers can be reheated, frozen or served as a salad the next day.

TIP: This is a super-quick dish when you use pre-cooked or leftover rice.

BREADS & BISCUITS

*B*reads and bis-
cuits, buttered
and flavored and
hot from the oven,
make any meal spe-
cial. Breads topped
with cheese or fix-
ings are ready in
15 minutes and hot
biscuits are ready in
20.

Quick Garlic Breadsticks

Complete the baking of packaged, pre-baked bread sticks as indicated on the package. Spread generously with butter or margarine and sprinkle with garlic salt. Serve immediately.

Cheese Bread Sticks

Cut pre-baked bread sticks in half lengthwise. Spread thinly with cheese spread or brush with olive oil. Sprinkle with a little grated medium Cheddar cheese and garlic salt. Bake as indicated on the package, or until the cheese is melted and lightly browned.

Cheesy Bread

Cut a baguette in half lengthwise. Cover with cheese spread and sprinkle with grated mozzarella. Bake at 425°F (220°C) until cheese melts and begins to brown, 8-10 minutes.

TIP: Use French bread slices, a bun or English muf-fin halves. This is also the best way to use up less than fresh bread. Delicious!

Grilled Cheese Bread

This recipe can be done in the oven or on the barbecue.

1	loaf French, or any dense crusty bread (use 12 slices)	1
2 tbsp.	olive oil	30 mL
2 cups	grated mozzarella OR pizza mix cheese	500 mL
4	plum tomatoes, chopped	4
½ tsp.	bottled, minced garlic or 1 clove minced	2 mL
1 tsp.	dried basil or ¼ cup (60 mL) chopped fresh sprinkling of pepper	5 mL

- Cut bread into 1" (2.5 cm) slices.

- Brush olive oil over both sides of the bread.

- Grill or toast 1 side of the bread.

- Meanwhile, lightly mix cheese, tomatoes, garlic and basil in a small bowl.

- Spread cheese mixture on the toasted side of the bread. Grill on the barbecue until the underside is toasted and the cheese melting. Or, toast both sides of the bread under the oven broiler. Spread cheese mixture on 1 side and return to the broiler until the cheese melts.

Makes 12 slices

Variation: For **Grilled or Baked Focaccia with Cheese and Herbs**, brush focaccia or any flatbread with 1 tsp. (5 mL) olive oil. Sprinkle with 1 tsp. (5 mL) Italian herb seasoning and 1 cup (250 mL) grated mozzarella. Grill in the oven or bake at 375°F (190°C) until heated through and the cheese melts, 12-15 minutes.

Pictured on page 17.

Quick Drop Biscuits

Both the plain and the cheese versions are my grandkids' favorites. Homemade soup calls for hot biscuits. Make a double batch so that you have a few days' supply. Reheat biscuits in the toaster oven or microwave.

2 cups	unbleached flour	500 mL
4 tsp.	baking powder	20 mL
1/2 tsp.	salt	2 mL
4 tbsp.	shortening OR solid margarine, chilled	60 mL
1 cup	skim milk (whole if you prefer)	250 mL

- Heat oven to 450°F (230°C). Lightly oil a cookie sheet or pizza pan.

- Combine flour, baking powder and salt in a medium-sized bowl. Stir with a whisk or fork to distribute baking powder and salt.

- Cut in shortening finely, using 2 knives or a pastry blender.

- Add milk and stir until combined.

- Using a large spoon, drop dough by rounded spoonfuls onto prepared pan. You will have 10-12 biscuits.

- Bake on the middle oven rack for 8-10 minutes.

Makes 10-12 biscuits

Variation: For **Cheddar Biscuits**, add 1/2-1 cup (125-250 mL) grated medium or aged Cheddar cheese. For **Spicy Cheddar**, add 1/4 tsp. (1 mL) cayenne or 1/2 tsp. (2 mL) red pepper flakes. For **Cheese Garlic Biscuits**, add 1/4 tsp. (1 mL) of garlic powder to the Cheddar Biscuits.

Variation: For **Herb Biscuits**, add 2 tbsp. (30 mL) chopped chives or green onions and 1 tsp. (5 mL) or so of dillweed or Italian Herbs. For a new taste try 1 tsp. (5 mL) herbes de Provence* and brush biscuit tops with melted butter.

* Herbes de Provence is a mixture that usually includes basil, marjoram, summer savory, thyme, sage, fennel seed and lavender.

Cheese Garlic Biscuits

Serve with soups and salads.

2 cups	biscuit baking mix (purchased or homemade)	500 mL
¾-1 cup	milk	175-250 mL
½ cup	grated Cheddar cheese (2 oz. [55 g])	125 mL
2 tbsp.	butter OR margarine, melted	30 mL
¼ tsp.	garlic powder	1 mL

- Heat oven to 450°F (230°C).

- Mix baking mix, ¾ cup (175 mL) milk and the cheese in a large bowl. Stir until moistened. You may need a little more milk. Dough should be soft. Do not overmix.

- Drop dough by spoonfuls onto an ungreased cookie sheet. (I use parchment paper – no pan to wash.)

- Bake for 10-12 minutes, until golden brown.

- Mix melted butter with garlic powder and brush over warm biscuits before removing from cookie sheet. Serve warm.

Makes 10-12 biscuits.

Variation: For **Herb Biscuits**, omit cheese and add ½ tsp. (2 mL) each of oregano, basil and thyme or 1 tsp. (5 mL) Italian herb mix to the biscuit mix. For **Herb Cheese Biscuits** use both the cheese and the herbs.

Variation: For **Spicy Cheddar Biscuits**, add ¼ tsp. (1 mL) cayenne or ½ tsp. (2 mL) red pepper flakes.

TIP: Recipe can be doubled.

TIP: For traditional round biscuits, lightly knead the dough on the counter; pat or roll into a circle and cut with a floured 2" (5 cm) round cookie/biscuit cutter.

Blueberry Muffins

In the summer at Setting Lake, near Thompson, Manitoba, we pick wild berries. A good blueberry season means pancakes, muffins and jam all winter. Here is the muffin recipe we like best.

2 cups	unbleached all-purpose flour	500 mL
4 tsp.	baking powder	20 mL
¹/₂ tsp.	salt	2 mL
¹/₄ cup	sugar	60 mL
1	egg	1
1 cup	milk	250 mL
¹/₄ cup	melted butter, margarine OR vegetable oil	60 mL
¹/₄ tsp.	nutmeg (optional)	1 mL
1 cup	fresh or frozen blueberries	250 mL

- Heat oven to 400°F (200°C).

- Lightly oil a muffin pan or line with paper cups.

- In a large bowl, combine flour, baking powder, salt and sugar.

- Break the egg into a separate bowl. Add milk, melted butter and nutmeg. Whisk until combined.

- Pour the milk mixture into the dry mixture. Stir until just combined. Add blueberries and stir lightly once or twice. A light touch and a minimum of mixing makes a tender muffin.

- Spoon the batter into muffin pan, filling cups to ²/₃ full. Bake 20-25 minutes.

Makes 12 medium muffins

Variation: For **Whole-Wheat Muffins**, use 1 cup (250 mL) unbleached flour and 1 cup (250 mL) whole-wheat flour.

Variation: To make **Cranberry Muffins**, use 1 cup (250 mL) of bog berries or cranberries. When using commercial berries, chop them up a bit.

Variation: For a change, top muffins with a sprinkling of cinnamon sugar.

MAIN MEALS

Main dish salads, pastas, eggs, beans, fish, chicken, pork, beef

Main Meals

These quick meals can be prepared in 30 minutes. They include fish, poultry, meat and other high-protein choices such as tofu, eggs and beans. Most are prepared from fast-cooking or pre-cooked ingredients, include fresh fruits or vegetables, and can be made from ingredients on hand.

When making meat choices, skinless, boneless **chicken** breasts and thighs are a good protein choice as they are tasty, low in fat and quick-cooking. Turkey comes packaged in meal-size portions of thighs and breasts, and also ground for patties and sauces.

Fish is also low in fat and quick to prepare. Frozen fish is very good in quality as it is usually frozen within a few hours of being caught. When using fresh fish find out when it is delivered to your market; purchase and use the same or the next day.

Beef and **pork** are part of many of our favorite dishes. To be healthwise, plan on 3-4 oz. per serving per person and choose lean cuts such as top sirloin, tenderloin chops and lean ground meats. Choosing these cuts means an increase in the cost per ounce, but not for the meal, as there is less waste.

Cooking **eggs** for dinner is quick and they bring protein, vitamins and minerals to our meals. For more variety and good health, we include tofu, beans, pasta and grains.

Here is a collection of new flavors and old favorites to enjoy.

Here is a selection of one-dish meals and grilled entrées that are a complete meal with the addition of a side dish. Meals from far away places tickle the taste buds and traditional favorites satisfy the soul. All are quick to cook and good tasting too.

Main Dish Salads

These salads are especially welcome on hot summer evenings. In the winter they are also satisfying and refreshing.

Side salads become whole meal salads when you add chicken, ham, tuna, eggs, beans or cheese. The meat can be precooked, barbecued, or stovetop grilled. A trip to the deli will provide some useful additions.

Count on the store cupboard to provide canned fish, beans and pasta, and the fridge for eggs and cheese.

Turkey or Chicken Salad with Fruit

Use leftover turkey or pre-cooked chicken for this dish. Include whatever fruits and vegetables you have on hand. The dressing is low fat and the curry adds just enough flavor so that you say "mmm that's good!"

6-8 cups	prepared mixed salad greens, add a little grated red cabbage OR broccoli slaw mix for color and texture	1.5-2 L
4 cups	cooked turkey or chicken, cut in 1/2" (1.3 cm) pieces	1 L
8 oz.	can pineapple tidbits, drained	250 g
1	celery stalk, diced	1
1/2 cup	coarsely chopped toasted pecans OR peanuts	125 mL

Creamy Dressing

1/2 cup	light mayonnaise	125 mL
1/4 cup	skim-milk yogurt	60 mL
1 tbsp.	lemon OR lime juice	15 mL
1 tsp.	curry powder	5 mL
1 tbsp.	chutney (optional) salt and pepper to taste	15 mL

- Prepare the salad greens.

- In a large bowl combine the turkey, pineapple, celery and pecans.

- Mix the dressing ingredients and toss with the turkey mixture.

- Serve the salad on individual plates. Line each plate with greens. Top with a serving of the turkey mixture and sprinkle with additional nuts.

Serves 4-6

Variation: Garnish each serving with additional fruit. Try apple slices or banana pieces dipped in lemon juice, apricots or prunes, or a canned peach half with a spoonful of chutney in the center.

Cobb Salad

In a restaurant in Santa Fe this beautiful salad was served on a platter. The crayon box colors and textures tempt the taste buds. Vary the ingredients according to what you like or have on hand. Allow up to ¼ lb. (125 g) of chicken or ham per person.

lettuce leaves OR coarsely chopped greens
cooked chicken OR turkey breast, diced
cooked ham, diced
bacon, cooked until crisp and crumbled
hard-boiled eggs, diced
green onions, chopped, tops also
blue cheese, OR cheese of choice, crumbled
ripe avocado, peeled and diced
cucumber, peeled, seeded and diced

- Line a large platter with lettuce leaves or coarsely chopped greens.
- Choose small amounts of 5 or 6 of the remaining ingredients.
- Place the individual ingredients side by side on the greens so that they resemble the rows of kernels on a cob of corn

Serve with a creamy, commercial dressing or use the dressing below:

Serves 4

Low-Fat Cucumber Dressing

½ cup	low-fat mayonnaise	125 mL
½ cup	skim milk yogurt OR buttermilk	125 mL
1	lime (use the juice and a little zest too if you have time)	1
¼ cup	peeled, seeded, chopped cucumber	60 mL
	salt and pepper to taste	

- Combine all ingredients and serve with the Cobb Salad or other salads.

Makes 1¼ cups (300 mL)

15-Minute Taco Salad

Vary the amounts in this layered salad to allow as many servings as you need. This is a super-quick version of the restaurant special.

½-1 lb.	lean ground beef	250-500 g
1	medium onion, chopped	1
½	green pepper, seeded and chopped	½
1 tbsp.	chili powder	15 mL
	salt and pepper to taste	
5 oz.	corn chips (approximately)	140 g
4 cups	lettuce, mixed greens preferred	1 L
3	plum tomatoes, chopped	3
2	green onions, sliced (including tops)	2
1 cup	grated cheese	250 mL
½ cup	chopped black olives	125 mL
	salsa	
	sour cream	

- In a large non-stick pan on medium-high heat, cook and stir the meat, onion and green pepper until the meat changes color and the vegetables are soft, about 5 minutes. Add the chili powder and a sprinkling of salt and pepper. Stir and cook 1-2 minutes.

- Spoon the meat mixture into a paper towel-lined bowl to cool a little. Blot with the towel to absorb the excess fat.

- Spread the corn chips on a serving platter. Layer the chips with lettuce, the meat mixture, tomatoes, onions, cheese, olives and salsa. Garnish with sour cream or put the salsa and sour cream in small bowls and serve as condiments.

Serves 4

Variation: Use as many or as few chips as you like, and try the recipe with tortilla or taco chips as well.

Pasta Salad with Veggies

Pasta salads are best with strong flavorings – second day servings are even tastier. I like the tang of cider vinegar in this recipe.

1½ cups	elbow OR small fusilli macaroni	375 mL
½ cup	low-fat mayonnaise	125 mL
¼ cup	skim-milk yogurt	60 mL
1 tbsp.	cider vinegar	15 mL
1 tbsp.	Dijon mustard	15 mL
1 tsp.	bottled minced garlic	5 mL
1 tsp.	sugar	5 mL
½ tsp.	salt	2 mL
¼ tsp.	pepper	1 mL
2	celery stalks, finely chopped	2
1 cup	chopped broccoli florets	250 mL
4	green onions, sliced (including some tops)	4
1	red pepper, seeded and chopped	1

- Cook pasta according to package directions. Drain. Rinse and drain again.

- Meanwhile, combine all the remaining ingredients in a large bowl. Add cooled pasta. Stir and toss.

Serves 4-6

Variation: Add a little more yogurt and 1 of the following: 1½ cups (375 mL) of cheese cubes, diced ham, a can of water-packed tuna flaked or ½ lb. (250 g) cubed deli fajita chicken.

Variation: For a buffet serving, or an attractive presentation, serve on a platter or a deep plate ringed with alternate slices of tomatoes and cucumber.

TIP: To cool pasta quickly, rinse under cold running water; add a few ice cubes as well.

PASTA

If salsa is the hottest (no pun intended) condiment in North America, pasta is the hottest dish. Hot, cold, quick or gourmet, pasta as a side or main dish, we like them all. You can cook the pasta separately and add the sauce or cook the vegetables with the pasta and add a little cheese or sauce.

Here are some great main-dish pasta sauces and pasta ideas:

Choose the Basic Tomato Sauce recipe, page 99 or your favorite commercial pasta sauce to serve with the long pastas like spaghetti and linguine. Sauces thick with meat and vegetables are best with shell and curly shapes, the twists and cups hold the chunky pieces.

Smaller portions of Summer Tomato Pasta, page 100, and Pasta and Vegetables, page 101, or cooked pasta tossed with a little olive oil and some herbs can be a side for chicken or other meats.

How much you cook depends on whether you are feeding fussy children or hungry teenagers and whether the pasta is a main dish or a side dish. The average recommendation is 1 pound (500 g) of pasta for 4 people.

Refrigerate leftovers and pack them for a cold lunch at work or reheat for another meal. To reheat, add a few tablespoons (45-60 mL) of sauce or water and cook for a few minutes in a covered pan on the stove.

To reheat pasta in the microwave, cook in a covered dish for 3-5 minutes on high.

Basic Tomato Sauce

A quick, fresh-tasting sauce for pasta. Try it also with a prepared filled pasta such as ravioli or tortellini.

2 tbsp.	olive oil	30 mL
1	medium onion, chopped AND/OR 2 garlic cloves, crushed	1
1	celery stalk, finely chopped	1
28 oz.	can diced tomatoes	796 mL
1 tbsp.	dried basil or ¼ cup (60 mL) chopped fresh	15 mL
	salt and pepper to taste	
¼ tsp.	dried hot pepper flakes (optional)	1 mL

- In a saucepan, heat oil over medium-high heat. Add onion, garlic (if using) and celery. Cook until soft, about 5 minutes.

- Add tomatoes, basil and pepper flakes, if using, and cook for 5 minutes. Season with salt and pepper and serve with the pasta of your choice.

Makes 3½ cups (875 mL), enough for up to 1 lb. (500 g) of pasta

Variation: For added flavor and nutrition, add 1 cup (250 mL) grated carrots to the pan with the celery. Stir and cook about 10 minutes before adding the tomato.

TIP: Purée or blend the sauce to hide the carrots from carrot haters.

Variation: For a **Mushroom Sauce**, add 2 cups (500 mL) sliced mushrooms to the pan after the onions have cooked a few minutes. Then add the tomatoes.

Variation: For **Pizza Spaghetti Sauce** combine the pasta and sauce. Add 1 cup (250 mL) grated Cheddar or mozzarella cheese and toss.

TIP: I like the flavor boost of a ¼ tsp. (1 mL) of dried pepper flakes added to the sauce.

Summer Tomato Pasta

Try this flavorful fresh pasta dish with grilled meat or fish. Prepare the sauce in minutes, set aside for a couple of hours at room temperature, serve with pasta or rice.

4	large garden tomatoes, diced	4
½ cup	peeled, seeded cucumber	125 mL
1	garlic clove, minced	1
¼ cup	chopped fresh basil OR 1 tbsp. (15 mL) dried	60 mL
¼ cup	chopped fresh mint or 1 tbsp. (15 mL) dried	60 mL
¼ cup	chopped fresh parsley	60 mL
2 tbsp.	olive oil	30 mL
½ tsp.	salt	2 mL
1 tsp.	sugar	5 mL
½ tsp.	pepper	1 mL
8 oz.	spaghetti OR linguine	250 g

- Place all of the ingredients, except the pasta, in a bowl and mix well. Let stand at room temperature for 2-4 hours.

- Cook the pasta in a large pot of boiling water until tender but firm. Drain and toss with the tomato sauce.

Serves 3-4

TIP: Leftovers are good cold or heated for 2 minutes in the microwave.

TIP: **Pasta Yields***

	Uncooked	Cooked	Servings
Macaroni	6-7 oz. (170-200 g)	4 cups (1 L)	4 to 6
Spaghetti	7-8 oz. (200-250 g)	4 cups (1 L)	4 to 6
Noodles	8 oz. (250 g)	4-5 cups (1-1.25 L)	4 to 6

* Appetites vary and the number of side dishes also determine the amount of pasta needed.

Pasta and Vegetables

The absence of garlic in this sauce emphasizes the vegetable flavors.

8 oz.	spaghetti, cooked	250 g
2 tbsp.	vegetable oil (use ½ butter for extra flavor!)	30 mL
1	medium or large onion, peeled and chopped	1
4 cups	vegetables, chopped into large pieces (use any combination of cauliflower, broccoli, zucchini, squash, celery, and mushrooms)	1 L
1 tsp.	Italian herb seasoning	5 mL
24 oz.	jar spaghetti sauce	680 mL
¼ tsp.	red pepper flakes	1 mL
¼ cup	freshly grated Romano OR Parmesan cheese	60 mL

- Cook the spaghetti according to package directions.

- In a large non-stick pan, heat the oil on medium-high.

- Add onions and sauté for about 2 minutes.

- Add the vegetables and the herb seasoning and sauté, turning/tossing for about 7 minutes, or until lightly browned and partially cooked.

- Add the spaghetti sauce and red pepper flakes. Bring to a boil. Stir and reduce to a simmer.

- Cook for 5 minutes more, or until vegetables are tender-crisp.

- Toss with drained pasta. Top with grated cheese.

Serves 4

TIP: For quicker cooking, use a 1 lb. (500 g) package of frozen vegetables. Do not brown. Add to the pan after the onions are cooked and when you add the spaghetti sauce.

TIP: For a flavor boost, try some of the new commercial spaghetti sauces, such as sundried tomato, 3-cheese or chunky garlic.

Greek Pasta with Beans, Tomatoes and Feta

From Brita Housez' book Tofu Mania – *very healthy and absolutely delicious.*

2 cups	uncooked pasta, penne OR rotini	500 mL
1 tbsp.	vegetable oil	15 mL
½	medium onion, coarsely chopped	½
2-3	garlic cloves, minced	2-3
4	sun-dried tomatoes, in oil, drained and coarsely chopped	4
19 oz.	can stewed tomatoes, drained, liquid reserved	540 mL
19 oz.	can white beans, rinsed and drained	540 mL
2 tbsp.	chopped fresh basil, cilantro OR parsley, OR a combination	30 mL
	generous pinch of dried oregano	
	salt OR soy sauce, to taste	
dash	cayenne pepper (optional)	dash
10 oz.	bag fresh spinach, shredded	285 mL
2 tbsp.	sliced black olives OR 8-10 whole olives	30 mL
1 cup	cubed medium or firm tofu*	250 mL
½ cup	crumbled feta cheese	125 mL

- Cook pasta according to package directions. Drain; keep warm.

- In a large, deep, non-stick frying pan, heat oil.

- Add onion, garlic and sun-dried tomatoes. Sauté 1 or 2 minutes.

- Add stewed tomatoes, beans, herbs and seasonings. Simmer on low for about 5 minutes. If mixture is dry, stir in some liquid from the stewed tomatoes. Add spinach. Cover and simmer another 3 to 5 minutes, or until spinach is wilted.

- Fold in olives and tofu. Adjust seasonings. Serve tomato/bean mixture over hot pasta and top with feta.

Serves 4-5

* If your family is not tofu-friendly, shred or grate the tofu and it will disappear into the sauce.

Tofu is free from saturated fat and cholesterol. It is made from protein rich soybeans and contains all 8 essential amino acids. It has a creamy smooth texture and much nutritional goodness.

Corkscrew Pasta with Tuna Vegetable Sauce

This is a new twist on an old standby.

8 oz.	corkscrew pasta (rotini, fusilli)	250 g
1 tsp.	vegetable oil, butter OR margarine	5 mL
2 cups	frozen mixed vegetables, thawed	500 mL
½ tsp.	bottled minced garlic OR 1 garlic clove, crushed	2 mL
10 oz.	can condensed cream of mushroom soup	284 mL
1 cup	milk	250 mL
1-1½ cups	grated mozzarella cheese	250-375 mL
2 x 4 oz.	cans solid white tuna packed in water, drained and flaked	2 x 113 g
	salt and pepper to taste	
1	small package potato OR tortilla chips (snack size)	1

- Cook pasta according to package directions. Drain and set aside.

- While the pasta is cooking, in a large sauce pan or non-stick skillet, heat the oil over medium-high heat. Add the vegetables and garlic. Stir and heat for about 3 minutes.

- Add soup, milk and cheese. Stir and heat to boiling. Reduce heat to low.

- Gently stir in the tuna, pasta and salt and pepper to taste. Heat for a few minutes.

- Serve in a large bowl and garnish with crushed potato or tortilla chips.

Serves 4

Variation: For a heartier cheese flavor, use sharp Cheddar cheese.

To speed up pasta preparation, put hot water in the pasta pot and put it onto the heat before you prepare the sauce. Add the salt after it boils. Salty water takes longer to boil.

- *Faster? Heat the water in two pots and combine when they boil.*

- *When you cook pasta and vegetables for the same meal, put the broccoli, cauliflower or thinly-sliced carrots with the cooking pasta for the last two minutes. Drain and sauce.*

Chicken Tomato Penne

Don't worry about the number of ingredients. They are the toss-in-kind. This is a quick dish.

8 oz.	penne or other small, ridged pasta	250 g
1 tbsp.	olive OR vegetable oil	15 mL
4	skinless, boneless chicken breasts, cut into ½" (1.3 cm) strips	4
1 tsp.	bottled minced garlic OR 2 cloves, crushed	5 mL
1	red bell pepper, seeded, cut into ½" (1.3 cm) pieces	1
1	yellow pepper, seeded, cut into ½" (1.3 cm) pieces	1
2	Roma tomatoes, thinly sliced	2
14 oz.	can crushed tomatoes OR diced tomatoes	398 mL
1 tsp.	dried basil	5 mL
½ tsp.	freshly ground black pepper	2 mL
2 tbsp.	lemon juice (fresh is best)	30 mL
	freshly grated Parmesan cheese	

- Cook pasta according to package directions.

- Meanwhile, in a large, non-stick pan, heat oil over medium-high heat. Add the chicken and cook until almost no pink remains, about 4 minutes. Add garlic and cook 1 minute more.

- Transfer chicken to a dish and cover.

- Add a little more oil to the pan. Add the peppers and cook and stir about 3 minutes.

- Add the tomato slices, chicken, canned tomatoes, basil, pepper and lemon juice. Bring to a boil; reduce heat and simmer for 5 minutes to blend flavors.

- Toss the cooked penne with the sauce and serve with Parmesan.

Serves 4-5

Variation: Substitute vegetables of your choice. Try thinly-sliced carrots, onions, broccoli florets, mushrooms or asparagus.

Mom's Goulash with Macaroni

As a child, Sunday meant roast beef and all the fixings. Monday supper was meat and gravy sandwiches or Goulash. Here is a ground beef version.

6 oz.	uncooked elbow macaroni about 2 cups (500 mL)	170 g
½ lb.	extra lean ground beef	250 g
1	small onion, chopped	1
½	green pepper, seeded and chopped	½
½ cup	water	125 mL
14 oz.	can diced tomatoes	398 mL
1 tsp.	bottled minced garlic	5 mL
1 tsp.	chili powder	5 mL
½-1 cup	cubed Cheddar cheese	125-250 mL

- Cook macaroni according to package directions; drain.

- Meanwhile, spray a large non-stick pan with cooking spray or oil. Add beef, onion and green pepper. Cook until the veggies are soft and the meat changes color.

- Add the remaining ingredients, except the macaroni and cheese. Bring to a boil. Reduce heat and simmer to heat through and combine flavors, about 5 minutes.

- Stir in macaroni and cheese. Heat for a few minutes more and serve

Serves 3-4

Variation: Use leftover beef or pork roast or yesterday's hamburgers, cut into chunks, in place of ground meat. The amount is not important. Be sure to add any leftover gravy.

Variation: Add vegetables of your choice, such as carrots, celery, corn or beans with the tomatoes. Cook a little longer, about 10 minutes.

To thaw a frozen block of spinach for a recipe, put the frozen spinach in a 2-quart (2 L) casserole in the microwave. Microwave on high for 3 minutes. Uncover. Cool slightly. Squeeze dry and chop.

Italian Sausage and Penne

The spinach is cooked with the pasta to make a colorful nutrient-loaded meal.

2¹⁄₂ cups	penne	625 mL
10 oz.	pkg. fresh spinach or frozen spinach, partially thawed and chopped, see tip page 105	283g
³⁄₄ lb.	mild Italian sausage (hot if you like)	340 g
1 tbsp.	vegetable oil	15 mL
1	onion, chopped	1
1	garlic clove, chopped	
1	red pepper, seeded and chopped	1
28 oz.	can meatless spaghetti sauce	796 mL
2 tsp.	dried basil	10 mL
1 cup	mozzarella OR provolone cheese, grated	250 mL

- In a large pot of boiling salted water cook pasta for 6 minutes.

- Add spinach and bring the water back to a boil; cook for 1 minute.

- Drain pasta and spinach and return it to the pot.

- Meanwhile, cut the sausage into ¹⁄₂" (1.3 cm) slices and cook in a large saucepan or Dutch oven over medium-high heat. Cook until done, about 5 minutes.

- Remove the meat and place on a paper-towel-lined plate, pat with another paper towel to remove excess fat.

- Drain and wipe out the pan. Reheat on medium-high heat. Add a little oil, onions, garlic and pepper. Cook, stirring occasionally, for about 4 minutes.

- Add the cooked meat, spaghetti sauce and basil to the vegetables in the pan; cook and stir until heated through.

- Combine sauce with penne and spinach; stir in cheese and serve.

Serves 4-6

Variation: For **Italian Chicken and Penne**, use skinless, boneless chicken thighs or breasts – cubed – in place of Italian sausage.

Variation: Substitute 3 cups (750 mL) of peeled, chopped broccoli for the spinach and cook in the same way, adding it to the pasta water near the end of cooking.

Crustless Spinach Cheddar Quiche

Ready for the oven in less than 10 minutes and cooked in 30. Crustless means less fat and less time – this spinach quiche is loaded with good food value. Serve it with an orange and romaine salad or sliced tomatoes.

3	eggs	3
1½ cups	milk or evaporated milk	375 mL
⅓ cup	all-purpose flour	75 mL
1 tsp.	baking powder	5 mL
½ tsp.	EACH salt and pepper	2 mL
¼ tsp.	ground nutmeg	1 mL
10 oz.	pkg. frozen chopped spinach, thawed drained and squeezed until most of the moisture is removed	283 g
1 cup	grated Cheddar OR Swiss cheese	250 mL
1	green onion, chopped (optional)	1
½	red pepper, chopped (optional)	½

- Preheat oven to 350°F (180°C).

- Oil a 9 x 9″ (23 x 23 cm) baking pan.

- Combine eggs and milk in a bowl; whisk to combine. Whisk in flour, baking powder, salt, pepper and nutmeg.

- Pour egg mixture into prepared pan. Distribute spinach and cheese evenly over the egg mixture; add onion and pepper, if using.

- Bake for 30 minutes, or until set at the edges but still jiggly in the middle.

Serves 3-4

Variation: For **Ham and Tomato Quiche**, substitute ½ cup (125 mL) chopped ham and ½ cup (125 mL) chopped, drained tomatoes for the spinach.

Variation: For **Broccoli Cheddar Quiche** use 1 cup (250 mL) chopped cooked broccoli in place of the spinach and use sharp Cheddar, not Swiss cheese.

2% evaporated milk is a good low-fat substitute for cream in sauces and baking. It gives a nutritional boost too.

Vegetable Garden Chili

There are many chili variations – this one is bursting with vegetables and topped with cheese. You can use the vegetables that you have on hand and change the bean combination. This recipe makes enough for a crowd or to freeze for leftovers.

2 tbsp.	olive OR vegetable oil	30 mL
3	celery stalks, chopped	3
1	green pepper, seeded and chopped	1
1-2	onion(s), peeled and chopped	1-2
2	garlic cloves, peeled and chopped	2
2 tbsp.	chili powder	30 mL
1 tsp.	cumin	5 mL
¼ tsp.	hot pepper flakes (optional)	1 mL
2	medium carrots, washed and chopped	2
2	potatoes, peeled and chopped	2
28 oz.	can plum tomatoes or diced tomatoes	796 mL
14-19 oz.	can black beans, drained and rinsed	398-540 mL
14-19 oz.	can kidney beans, drained and rinsed	398-540 mL
½-1 cup	chopped cashews (optional)	125-250 mL
1 tsp.	salt	5 mL
	grated Cheddar cheese	

- Assemble all the ingredients, put the ingredients listed in the first group (up to and including the pepper flakes) in a large saucepan over medium-high heat. Cook and stir until the onions are translucent, about 5 minutes.

- Stir in the rest of the ingredients, except cheese. Bring to a boil. Reduce heat and simmer 15 minutes or up to 60 minutes, until carrots and potatoes are tender.

- Serve in bowls, topped with grated cheese. Serve with toasted whole-wheat bread or garlic toast.

Serves 10 – makes 10 cups (2.5 L)

Slow Cooker Method: Omit the oil and put all the ingredients in a slow cooker. Cook 6-8 hours on low setting.

Variations: For **Tofu Chili** add chunks of grated firm tofu to the garlic, onion, spice mixture. For **Chicken Chili**, add ½-1 lb. (250-500 g) ground chicken or turkey to garlic, onion, spice mixture. Cook until the chicken is no longer pink, about 10 minutes.

TIP: To save time, coarsely grate potatoes and carrots.

TIP: Leftover chili means lunches and snacks – use as a sandwich filling with lettuce; top baked potatoes; wrap in a tortilla.

Salmon with Butter Dill Sauce

Lightly steamed in a non-stick pan, it is a feast for the eye and the palate.

1 tbsp.	vegetable oil	15 mL
4	salmon steaks, about 1" (2.5 cm) thick	4
½	lemon	½
1 tsp.	dried dillweed or ¼ cup (60 mL) chopped fresh dillweed	5 m
	salt and pepper	

- Heat the oil in a non-stick cooking pan over medium-high heat.

- Squeeze the lemon over both sides of the salmon steaks. Sprinkle with the dillweed and press it into the fish.

- Lightly brown each side of the fish, about 4 minutes. Season with salt and pepper.

- Reduce heat to low. Cover the pan and cook 6-8 minutes more.

- Check after about 5 minutes. If the fish is nicely browned, turn it over and continue cooking with the lid on.

- Serve as is or with Butter Dill Sauce.

Serves 4

Butter Dill Sauce

3 tbsp.	butter	45 mL
2 tsp.	lemon juice	10 mL
½ tsp.	EACH dried dillweed and parsley	2 mL

Cream all the ingredients together and spread over the cooked fish.

TIP: Fish takes about 10 minutes per inch (2.5 cm), measured at the thickest part, to cook when pan-fried, steamed or baked in a very hot (450°F [230°C]) oven. Fish is cooked when it is opaque and flakes easily with a fork.

CHICKEN

The mild flavor of chicken embraces herbs, spices, fruits and vegetables. I serve it hot, cold or at room temperature. Chopped or diced in a recipe, it cooks in 5 minutes. Flattened breasts or thighs are ready in 8-10 minutes. When preparing dinner, I often cook extra, store it in the freezer and know that I have the basis for a super-quick meal or sandwich.

Orange Soy Ginger Garlic Marinade for Chicken

This is nice when the chicken breast tops a green salad. Use this marinade for chicken breasts or thighs – grill, barbecue or bake.

⅓ cup	orange juice concentrate	75 mL
2 tbsp.	vegetable oil	30 mL
1 tbsp.	soy sauce	15 mL
1 tsp.	bottled minced garlic	5 mL
1 tsp.	bottled minced ginger	5 mL

- Mix the ingredients in a small bowl. Add to the chicken in a covered dish or plastic bag. Marinate, turning occasionally, for 15 minutes at room temperature or up to 24 hours in the fridge.

TIP: Chicken and marinade can be put in a self-closing plastic bag in the morning, ready for quick dinner fixings in the evening.

TIP: For quick no-fuss cooking, try the oven method on page 57.

Grilled Chicken

This is a basic recipe. Serve with rice or use the cooked chicken breasts to top a green salad or cut them lengthwise and make a chicken burger.

4	boneless, skinless chicken breasts	4
	Orange Soy Ginger Garlic Marinade, page 110, OR	
	see the quick marinade below	

- To flatten chicken breasts, place between 2 layers of waxed paper and pound with a meat mallet or rolling pin until flattened to an even thickness, about ½" (1.3 cm).

- Marinate for 15 minutes.

- Heat stove-top grill or barbecue to medium-high.

- Grill 4-5 minutes per side, until meat is tender but still moist.

- Cut in half lengthwise to make 2 thin slices from each breast or use as is.

- To serve, make chicken burgers with tomato slices, mayonnaise and lettuce OR slice the breasts diagonally and top a green salad that includes oranges and cucumbers. Pass a citrusy dressing.

Serves 4

Quick Marinade

For a super quick marinade, use ¼ cup (60 mL) Italian salad dressing with a tbsp. (15 mL) of lemon juice and a dash of black pepper.

TIP: When you have no time to marinate the chicken, brush the breasts with oil and sprinkle with herbs or seasoning salt and pepper; bake, grill or broil.

Individually frozen chicken breasts are an answer to a hurried cook's prayer. It takes about 10 minutes on the defrost cycle to defrost 4 boneless chicken breasts. To partially thaw a chicken breast, zap for 30-60 seconds on high.

- *To thaw frozen chicken breasts that are in a solid clump, run under hot water to separate and microwave on high for 2 minutes to start thawing.*

Chicken Vegetable Casserole with Cheddar Sauce

Assembled in minutes, this dish is a good choice for leftover chicken or turkey. The curry adds just a hint of flavor. To prepare from fresh chicken, cook as directed in the TIP below.

2-3 cups	cubed, cooked chicken OR turkey	500-750 mL
1 lb.	pkg. frozen California-style vegetables, thawed and chopped	500 g

Curried Cheddar Sauce

10 oz.	can cream of chicken soup	284 mL
1/2 cup	milk OR cream	125 mL
1 tsp.	curry powder	5 mL
1/4 cup	apple juice OR white wine	60 mL
1 cup	grated Cheddar cheese	250 mL

- Preheat oven to 375°F (190°C).

- Combine chicken/turkey and thawed vegetables in a 2 1/2-quart (2.5 L) oven-safe casserole.

- To make the sauce, combine soup, milk, curry and juice in a microwave-safe glass bowl. Cook on high until heated through, about 5 minutes. Stir twice

- Add the sauce to the chicken and vegetables in the casserole

- Top with grated cheese and bake 15-20 minutes, until cheese is melted and the sauce is bubbly and heated through

- Serve with rice or over hot biscuits or croissants

Serves 4

Variation: Golden Mushroom, Broccoli Cheddar and Cream of Chicken soups can be used for a flavor change. Or, try Cream of Asparagus soup and add drained, canned asparagus.

TIP: To cook chicken, cut 1 lb. (500 g) boneless, skinless chicken breasts or thighs into 1" (2.5 cm) chunks. Cook in 1 tbsp. (15 mL) vegetable oil over medium-high heat until chicken is tender and no pink remains, about 5 minutes. Toss and turn chicken while it cooks.

Chicken Paella

Saffron is the key to the exotic flavor and aroma of paella. This pared-down, quick version cooks the rice and other ingredients separately.

1 cup	long-grain rice	250 mL
2 cups	chicken broth (canned or reconstituted granules)	500 mL
¼ tsp.	saffron	1 mL
2 tbsp.	vegetable oil OR olive oil	30 mL
3	boneless, skinless chicken breasts, cut into bite-sized pieces	3
1	medium onion, chopped	1
2 tsp.	bottled minced garlic	10 mL
14 oz.	can diced tomatoes	398 mL
¼ tsp.	red pepper flakes	1 mL
4.5 oz.	can shrimp, drained and rinsed	128 g
1 cup	small frozen peas	250 mL
	salt and pepper to taste	
2	green onions, chopped	2

- In a medium-sized pot, bring rice, broth and saffron to a boil. Reduce heat to low and cook 15-20 minutes.

- While the rice is cooking, heat oil in a large non-stick pan over medium-high heat. Add chicken, toss and cook until the chicken begins to brown, 3-4 minutes. Add onion and garlic and continue cooking until the chicken is cooked through and lightly browned, 3-4 minutes.

- Add tomatoes and pepper flakes. Bring to a boil. Reduce heat and simmer for 3 minutes. Add shrimp and peas. Cover and heat, about 3 minutes. Taste and adjust seasoning. To serve, spread the rice on a large platter and top with the chicken mixture. Garnish with the green onion.

Serves 3-4

Variation: For larger servings, cook 4 chicken breasts or add ½ lb. (250 g) of sliced, cooked mild Italian sausage.

TIP: Saffron is the world's most expensive spice. It adds color and aroma to rice, fish and chicken dishes and a little goes a long way. Look for it in the specialty section of supermarkets and European, Middle Eastern and East Indian import stores.

Country Chicken

This is comfort food made simply and quickly. I like it best with mashed potatoes.

4	boneless, skinless chicken breasts, about 1 lb. (500 g)	4
¼ cup	flour	60 mL
2 tbsp.	vegetable oil	30 mL
1	onion, chopped	1
1	medium carrot, diced	1
2	celery stalks, chopped	2
1 tsp.	thyme	5 mL
2 cups	chicken broth, vegetable broth OR milk	500 mL
1 tbsp.	flour	15 mL
	salt and pepper to taste	
1 cup	frozen peas	250 mL

- Cut chicken in bite-sized pieces; put in a small bowl and coat with flour.

- In a large non-stick pan, heat oil over medium-high heat. Shake excess flour from the chicken pieces and cook until lightly browned.

- Add onions, carrots, celery and thyme. Cook and stir for 3 minutes.

- Mix 1 tbsp. flour with broth or milk and add to meat. Stir.

- Bring to a boil; reduce heat and simmer for 5 minutes.

- Season with salt and pepper. Add peas, reheat and serve.

Serves 4

Variation: For the flavors of Provence with the Country Chicken, use a 14 oz. (398 mL) can of diced tomatoes instead of broth, omit the 1 tbsp. (15 mL) flour add 1 tsp. (5 mL) bottled minced garlic or 2 crushed cloves, sautéed mushrooms, 1 tsp. (5 mL) basil and ½ tsp. (2 mL) rosemary.

Variation: For an Italian twist, add 14 oz. (398 mL) can of diced tomatoes instead of broth, omit the 1 tbsp. (15 mL) of flour and add 1 tsp. (5 mL) EACH of oregano and basil.

TIP: Boneless, skinless chicken thighs may be used instead of breasts.

Chicken Curry

I love the smell of curry. This dish has just a hint of far east flavor. Take a few minutes to prepare little dishes of condiments or serve as is.

2 tbsp.	vegetable oil	30 mL
³/₄ lb.	boneless, skinless chicken thighs	340 g
¹/₄ cup	flour	60 mL
1	onion, chopped	1
1 tbsp.	curry powder	15 mL
1 tsp.	ground cumin	5 mL
1 cup	coconut milk	250 mL
1 cup	chicken broth OR water	250 mL
2	medium potatoes, cubed	2
1	large carrot, thinly sliced or coarsely grated	1
1	apple, cored and chopped (skin on)	1
	salt and pepper to taste	
¹/₂ cup	chopped peanuts	125 mL

- Cut the chicken in bite-sized pieces and coat with flour

- Heat the oil in a large saucepan or Dutch oven over medium-high heat.

- Shake the excess flour off the chicken and lightly brown, about 5 minutes. Stir-fry, add onion; cook and stir about 2 minutes

- Push chicken and onion to the side and add curry powder and cumin to the middle. Stir and cook until browned and fragrant, 1-2 minutes, do not burn. This releases the full flavor of the spices

- Stir in coconut milk and broth, potatoes, carrots and apple. Bring the sauce to a boil. Reduce heat to a simmer. Cover and cook until potatoes are tender, about 10 minutes. Add salt and pepper to taste.

- Sprinkle with chopped peanuts and serve with rice and chutney

Serves 4-6

Pictured on the front cover.

Variations: For a more intense curry flavor, use 2 tbsp. (30 mL) curry powder and ¹/₄-¹/₂ tsp. (1-2 mL) dried red pepper flakes and/or try a 14 oz. (398 mL) can of diced tomatoes in place of coconut milk and broth.

Variation: Curry is a truly memorable dish when served with little dishes of condiments. To the chutney and peanuts add raisins, chopped banana, oranges and grapefruit, sliced green onions, chopped cucumber and red onion and grated coconut. Pile these on top of the rice and curry and enjoy the flavors that each forkful brings.

Chicken Vegetable Stir-Fry

This dish is so quick to cook you will need to have pasta or rice ready.

cooked pasta OR rice

Garlic Ginger Sauce:

2 tbsp.	soy sauce	30 mL
3 tbsp.	oyster sauce	45 mL
1 tbsp.	bottled minced garlic	15 mL
2 tsp.	bottled minced ginger	10 mL
1 tbsp.	rice wine vinegar OR cider vinegar	15 mL
2 tbsp.	ketchup	30 mL
1 tsp.	sesame oil	5 mL
1/2 cup	water OR chicken broth	125 mL
1 tbsp.	cornstarch	15 mL
1 tbsp.	vegetable oil	15 mL
3	skinless, boneless chicken breasts or 6 chicken thighs, cut into 1/4" (1 mL) strips	3
3-4 cups	chopped fresh vegetables, try onion, broccoli, red and green pepper, thinly sliced carrots and celery OR 1 lb. (500 g) bag of frozen oriental-style vegetables, partially thawed, chopped	750 mL-1 L
1/4 cup	water OR chicken stock	60 mL

- Prepare the pasta or rice.

- Combine all sauce ingredients in a small bowl.

- Heat the oil in a large, non-stick skilled over medium-high heat. Add the chicken; stir and cook until no pink remains, 3-4 minutes. Transfer chicken to a plate and cover.

- Add the vegetables to the pan; stir and toss. Add water or chicken broth and cover, reduce heat and steam until vegetables are tender crisp, about 2 minutes. Return chicken to pan. Mix well.

- Stir sauce; add to chicken mixture. Cook and stir until hot and sauce is thick and glossy, 2-4 minutes.

Serves 4

Variation: For **Ginger Orange Chicken,** replace half the chicken stock with orange juice; add 1/4 tsp. (1 mL) dried pepper flakes, 1 tsp. (5 mL) of grated orange rind and 1 tbsp. (15 mL) of hoisin sauce.

TIP: When you are comfortable with the stir-fry method, you can cook endless variations. Have sauces and vegetables prepared before you begin to cook.

Sweet and Sour Pineapple Chicken

This is sweet and sour and super quick, as the chicken is added to the sauce without browning the meat. Serve with rice.

8 oz.	can unsweetened pineapple tidbits or pineapple pieces cut in half, drained	250 mL
1/4 cup	white vinegar	60 mL
1 tbsp.	honey OR sugar	15 mL
2 tbsp.	soy sauce	30 mL
1 cup	chicken broth OR water	250 mL
1/8 tsp.	ground ginger	0.5 mL
3	boneless, skinless chicken breasts	3
1	onion, sliced thinly	1
2	celery stalks, sliced thinly	2
1	green pepper, seeded and sliced	1
3 tbsp.	cornstarch	45 mL
1/4 cup	chicken broth OR water	60 mL
	salt and pepper to taste	

- To make the sauce, combine the juice drained from the pineapple and the vinegar, honey, soy sauce, broth and ginger in a pot and heat.

- While the sauce is heating, cut the chicken into bite-sized pieces; add to the sauce.

- Bring to a boil. Add onions, celery and peppers. Return pot to a boil. Reduce heat and simmer for 5 minutes. Add pineapple pieces.

- Mix cornstarch and water in a small bowl or cup. Stir into the sauce, stirring. Bring to a boil and cook for 1 minute, until sauce is thickened and clear. Season and serve.

Serves 4

TIP: For more vegetables and more color, add chopped red pepper and a small carrot, coarsely grated.

PORK & BEEF

We eat less red meat now than in the past, but these meat choices remain excellent sources of iron. Today's products are very lean. For good nutrition, reduce serving sizes. Allow 2-4 oz. (55-115 g) per person and round out the meal with 3 or 4 vegetable choices.

Choosing Cuts of Meat

For beef, choose lean cuts such as loin, sirloin, and strip loin steaks, all round steak and roast cuts and rib eyes. Use lean and extra lean ground beef, cook well, drain and blot with paper towels to remove any excess fat. **For pork**, choose loin cuts, leg portions and the tenderloin.

The new packaging used by supermarkets is very helpful. The cut, preparation and cooking method are often included in the labeling. The meat case displays the cuts according to cooking methods: fry/sauté, grill/broil, roast/bake. The butchers in the meat department are there to answer your questions, to custom cut portions or repackage your choice if you wish.

Marinades add extra flavor and tenderness to pork, beef and poultry. You should always have a marinade on hand. Prepared salad dressings work well as does wine or cider mixed with a little garlic and herbs. Marinate for four hours or over night.

• Use the microwave to thaw or pre-cook meats, roasts and vegetables.

Szechuan Pork Stir-Fry

A quick dish with the fresh taste of orange and a spicy marinade.

Soy Ginger Marinade

1/4 cup	soy sauce	60 mL
2 tbsp.	brown sugar	30 mL
1 tbsp.	vegetable oil	15 mL
1	garlic clove, minced	1
1 tsp.	grated or minced ginger root	5 mL
1/2 tsp.	dried red pepper flakes	2 mL

Orange Sauce

1/3 cup	orange juice	75 mL
3 tbsp.	water	45 mL
1 1/2 tsp.	cornstarch	7 mL
1 lb.	pork strips or pork loin cut into 1/2" (1.3 cm) strips	500 g
1 tbsp.	vegetable oil	15 mL
4 cups	prepared vegetables of choice (sliced carrots, onions, celery, broccoli, cauliflower, red or green pepper and onion)	1 L

- To make the marinade, combine soy sauce, sugar, oil, garlic, ginger and dried pepper flakes in a ziplock bag; add pork and marinate at room temperature for 20-30 minutes or for up to 10 hours in the fridge.

- For sauce, combine juice, water and cornstarch in small bowl. Set aside.

- In a large skillet, stir-fry pork and marinade over medium-high heat until cooked. Meat will be tender with slight traces of pink. Transfer meat to a bowl and cover.

- Wipe out pan and add 1 tbsp. (15 mL) oil. Heat on medium-high, add vegetables and stir-fry until tender-crisp, about 5 minutes.

- Stir sauce mixture and pour into the center of the pan. Cook and stir until the sauce thickens. Add meat and accumulated juices. Stir and toss until the meat and vegetables are coated with sauce and heated through. Serve with rice.

Serves 4

Oyster sauce, hoisin sauce, stir-fry sauce and Asian black bean sauce are similar and can be interchanged if you don't have one of them on hand.

French Country Stew

This combination of flavors is so good, even those who claim they don't like fruit with their meat dishes love it.

³/₄ lb.	pork loin or chops cut into ³/₄" (2 cm) cubes	340 g
¹/₄ cup	flour	60 mL
1 tbsp.	vegetable oil	15 mL
1	medium onion, chopped	1
1	medium carrot, thinly sliced	1
1	celery stalk, thinly sliced (optional)	1
1 cup	sliced mushrooms (optional)	250 mL
2 tbsp.	flour	30 mL
2 cups	chicken broth OR water	30 mL
1	green apple, cut into ¹/₂" (1.3 cm) pieces	1
¹/₄ cup	raisins	60 mL
1 tsp.	rosemary	5 mL

- Coat pork pieces with flour. Heat oil in a large, non-stick pan over medium-high heat. Add pork pieces, stir and cook until the pork changes color and begins to brown, about 4 minutes.

- Add the onion, carrot, celery and mushrooms. Stir and cook for about 3 minutes.

- Stir in the flour until it is absorbed, about 2 minutes. Stir in broth.

- Add apples and raisins. Crush rosemary with your fingers or a knife blade and add to stew. Bring to a boil; reduce heat and simmer a few minutes, until apples are heated through.

Serves 3-4

Variation: Use chicken if you prefer **Chicken Stew**.

Variation: For **Pork Fricassee**, omit mushrooms and rosemary. Sauté 1 garlic clove, crushed, with the onion mixture. Add flour and stock or 2 cups (500 mL) of milk and proceed as above. Add salt and pepper to taste.

Pork Loin Chops

Pork loin chops, quickly cooked, are tender and delicious. Serve as is with applesauce or make a vegetable herb sauce. Choose chops that are $1/2$-1" (1.3-2.5 cm) thick.

2 tbsp.	vegetable oil	30 mL
4	pork loin chops at least $1/2$" (1.3 cm) thick	4
	sprinkling of pepper, dried thyme, rosemary and garlic or a commercial meat seasoning	

- Heat oil in a non-stick cooking pan over medium-high heat.

- Season the meat with the pepper and herbs , rubbing them into the meat. Brown the chops on both sides, about 5 minutes.

- Reduce the heat to medium and continue cooking until golden brown and cooked through, about 4 minutes per side.

Serves 4

Variation: For a **Vegetable Herb Sauce,** move the meat from the pan to a plate and cover. Reduce pan heat to medium, add 1 cup (250 mL) – combined amount – of chopped carrots, onion and celery to the pan. Cook until lightly browned, about 5 minutes. Add a cup (250 mL) of broth or water, $1/2$ tsp. (2 mL) rosemary, salt and pepper. Bring to a boil; reduce heat and simmer, stirring until combined and slightly reduced. Serve over chops.

For best results, don't overcook pork. It is much leaner now than in the past. It tastes best when cooked just until pink in the center.

- *To test for doneness, make a small cut in the thickest part of the chop. The juices should be clear and the meat slightly pink in color.*

- *For quick no-mess cooking, try the oven-cooked pork chops on page 58.*

Pork Medallions with Lemon

Pork loin is quick-cooking and very tender with no waste. Here the medallions are served with a lemony sauce.

3 tbsp.	vegetable oil OR butter	45 mL
1/4 cup	all-purpose flour	60 mL
1	pork loin, about 3/4 lb. (340 g), cut into 1" (2.5 cm) slices and flattened slightly with your hand or a meat mallet	1
	salt and pepper to taste	
2 cups	sliced mushrooms	500 mL
1/2 cup	chicken broth OR white wine	125 mL
2 tbsp.	lemon juice (the juice of 1/2 a lemon)	30 mL
1/2 cup	cream	125 mL
	parsley OR chopped green onion tops for garnish	

- Heat 2 tbsp. (30 mL) of oil or butter in a large, non-stick pan over medium-high heat.

- Put flour in a bowl. Dip pork into flour to coat both sides.

- Add the meat to the pan and cook quickly, 2-3 minutes on each side. Sprinkle with salt and pepper. Remove meat to a plate and cover.

- Add a little more oil to the pan. Add mushrooms and stir-fry, 4-5 minutes. Add broth or wine and lemon juice. Stir to combine and cook until heated through.

- Return meat to the pan. Stir. Cook until heated through.

- Reduce heat; add cream and heat gently. Do not boil.

- Garnish with a little chopped parsley or chopped onion tops and thin lemon slices. Serve.

Serves 3

TIP: *A pork tenderloin weighs about 3/4 lb. (365 g) and makes 3 servings. Cook more if needed or cook extra to make fajitas or bunwiches.*

Glazed Ham Steak

Serve with deli potato salad and coleslaw for a very quick meal.

1	ham steak, ³/₄" (2 cm) thick, about 1½ lbs.(750 g)	1

Orange Mustard Glaze

2 tbsp.	brown sugar	30 mL
2 tsp.	Dijon mustard	10 mL
2 tbsp.	frozen orange juice concentrate	30 mL

• Preheat the broiler and set the rack so that the ham steak is about 2" (5 cm) from the element. For easy clean up, spray the pan with cooking spray or line with aluminum foil.

• Mix sugar, mustard and orange juice together. Brush the steak with the glaze and broil 5-7 minutes each side. Continue to brush the steak as it cooks.

• Ham steak should be nicely browned and heated through.

Serves 4

Variation: To make an **Apricot Glaze**, mix 2 tbsp. (30 mL) of apricot jam, 1 tbsp. (15 mL) of vinegar (try cider) and ¼ tsp. (1 mL) of cinnamon in a cup or small dish, microwave and stir until liquid and well mixed. Brush on steak as above.

TIP: To prepare the ham in a non-stick skillet, heat the pan over medium-high heat. Add 1 tbsp. (15 mL) of vegetable oil. Cook the meat until lightly browned, about 5 minutes on each side. Heat Orange Mustard Glaze or Apricot Glaze and serve as a sauce.

Fajitas: Beef, Pork or Chicken

Fajitas are delicious and fun to eat. 2-4oz. (55-115 g) of meat per serving is ample.

2 tbsp.	lime juice or the juice of 1 lime	30 mL
1 tsp.	chili powder	5 mL
1/2 tsp.	cumin	2 mL
1/2- 1 lb.	boneless top sirloin, chicken OR pork	250-500 g
1	green pepper, seeded and sliced	1
1	red pepper, seeded and sliced	1
1	onion, sliced	1
2 tbsp.	vegetable oil, divided	30 mL
	salt and pepper to taste	
8	7" (18 cm) OR 4,10" (25 cm) tortillas	8

- In a small bowl, mix lime juice, chili powder and cumin.
- Cut the meat in 1/2" (1.3 cm) strips and add to the lime juice mixture. Set aside for a few minutes or place in the fridge for up to 8 hours.
- Heat 1 tbsp. (15 mL) of the oil in a large non-stick pan over medium-high heat. Drain the meat; pat dry with a paper towel; add to the pan. Stir and toss until cooked, 7-10 minutes. Add salt and pepper. Remove to a plate and cover.
- Wipe the pan clean with a paper towel. Add 1 tbsp. (15 mL) vegetable oil, heat over medium-high heat. Add peppers and onion. Cook until lightly browned, about 5 minutes. Add meat and juices to pan; reheat.
- Meanwhile, heat tortillas in the oven or microwave (see pkg. directions).
- Fill each tortilla with the meat and vegetable mixture. Roll and serve with sour cream, salsa and salad.

Serves 4

Variation: To serve fajitas in the traditional way, place the meat and vegetables on a heated plate or platter, wrap warmed tortillas in a large cloth napkin or tea towel; put the condiments on a plate or platter. Everyone prepares their own fajita, rolling the meat, vegetables and condiments into the tortilla. Choose 1 cup (250 mL) each of shredded lettuce, Cheddar cheese, chopped tomatoes, plus 1/2 cup (125 mL) of chopped red or green onion and small bowls of salsa and sour cream. Eat with a knife and fork if you choose – they taste best rolled and eaten out of hand, hot-dog style. Be sure to fold 1 edge up when rolling – to form a pocket.

Variation: Marinate 3/4-1 lb. (340-500 g) sirloin steak or chicken in lime and spices for at least 1/2 hour, turning 2 or 3 times. Grill on high until medium rare and well browned on the outside. Cook onions and peppers separately. To serve, slice steak thinly and top with vegetables. Serve with tortillas and condiments as previously described.

Teriyaki Steak

Choose your favorite cut of beef and allow 4-6 oz. (115-170 g) per person.

Teriyaki Marinade

¼ cup	hoisin sauce	60 mL
1 tbsp.	vinegar	15 mL
1 tbsp.	lemon OR lime juice	15 mL
2 tsp.	bottled, minced garlic, or 2 cloves, crushed	10 mL
1 tbsp.	bottled, minced ginger, or 1 tbsp., grated	15 mL
1 lb.	grilling steak*	500 g

- Combine the marinade ingredients in a sealable bag. Add the steak. Do this at night or in the morning. If you are short of time, 20-30 minutes will do. Turn the bag now and then so that all the meat comes in contact with the marinade.

- Remove the steak from the marinade. Pat dry with a paper towel.

- Preheat grill pan or non-stick frying pan on medium-high. Coat with oil or cooking spray.

- Cook meat 5-7 minutes per side for medium rare.

- To barbecue, cook 5-7 minutes per side over medium-high heat.

Serves 2-4, depending on appetites

* Suitable grilling steaks would be strip loin, rib eye and inside round.

Variation: Barbecued Teriyaki Steak can be served as is with rice and salad or thinly sliced and served on top of salad.

Variation: Barbecuing is an alternate method for cooking steak or chicken for Fajitas.

For steak; marinate the meat in a mixture of 2 tbsp. (30 mL) lime juice, 1 tsp. (5 mL) chili powder and ½ tsp. (2 mL) cumin for ½ hour or up to 8 hours – turn now and then. Grill on high until medium rare and well-browned. Cook onions and peppers separately in a pan or brush lightly with oil and grill or barbecue.

For chicken; marinate boneless chicken breasts or thighs as above and cook over medium heat until chicken is cooked through, with no remaining pink color, but still tender and juicy. Serve with tortillas and condiments as described on page 124.

TIP: Place the self-closing bag containing the steak on a plate as sometimes the bags leak.

Tomato Beef Curry

This recipe cooks very quickly. Be sure to have the ingredients prepared and the cornstarch, broth and soy sauce mixed together and ready to add at the end.

1 tbsp.	vegetable oil	15 mL
¾-1 lb.	grilling steak, cut into ¼" (1 cm) slices	365-500 g
1	medium onion, halved and sliced	1
1	green pepper, seeded and sliced	1
2	garlic cloves, minced	2
1 tsp.	dried ginger	5 mL
2 tbsp.	curry powder	30 mL
6	Roma tomatoes, cut in ¼" (1 cm) wedges	6
1 cup	beef broth OR water	250 mL
2 tbsp.	soy sauce	30 mL
1 tbsp.	cornstarch	15 mL
	sprinkling of black pepper	

- In a large, non-stick pan, heat oil over medium-high heat. Add the steak, ½ at a time, and cook until meat changes color but is still pink in the middle, 2-3 minutes. Add a little more oil if necessary. Remove the meat to a plate and cover.

- Heat 1 tsp. of oil in the pan. Add onion and green pepper. Cook and stir until soft, about 2 minutes.

- Add garlic, ginger and curry powder to the center of the pan. Cook and stir for 1 minute.

- Add tomato wedges. Cook and stir until heated through, about 3 minutes. Add water or broth. Return the meat to the pan and heat a little.

- Combine broth, soy sauce and cornstarch. Stir into the liquid in the pan. Heat and stir until the sauce thickens and the meat and vegetables are coated with the sauce. Serve with rice.

Serves 4

TIP: The sliced Roma tomatoes peppers and onions add color and texture to this dish. A 14 oz. (398 mL) can of diced tomatoes can be substituted for the Romas if you prefer.

Cube Steaks* with Mushroom Gravy

Two, four, six. Buy as many tenderized steaks as you have people to serve. Mashed or baked potatoes and salad are what I like with this dinner.

2 tbsp.	vegetable oil	30 mL
4	cube steaks*	4
½ tsp.	seasoning salt and a sprinkle of pepper	2 mL
1	onion, chopped	1
½ lb.	fresh mushrooms, sliced	250 g
2 tbsp.	flour	30 mL
½ tsp.	thyme	2 mL
1½-2 cups	1% OR 2% milk	375-500 mL
	salt and pepper to taste	

- Heat 1 tbsp. (15 mL) of oil in a large, non-stick pan over medium-high heat.

- Brown steaks on both sides. Sprinkle with seasoning salt and a little pepper. Remove to a plate and cover.

- Add a little more oil to the pan. Add onions and mushrooms. Cook and stir until soft, 3-4 minutes.

- Stir in flour and thyme. Mix and stir until blended, about 1 minute. Add milk a little at a time, stirring as you do. Bring to a boil. Add meat. Spoon gravy over meat and cook until heated through, 3-5 minutes. Season with salt and pepper.

Serves 4

* Cube steaks are top or bottom round steaks that have been tenderized by a butcher.

Variation: Instead of cube steaks, use pork tenderloin flattened into medallions or pork cutlets. Pork tenderloin will cook in 2-3 minutes.

Variation: Cook pork quick-fry chops and add 1 tsp. (5 mL) dried herbes de Provence in place of thyme. Core and slice a Granny Smith apple; add with the mushrooms.

Beef Stroganoff

Canned soup makes a quick meal of this long-time favorite.

2 tbsp.	vegetable oil	30 mL
1 lb.	boneless top sirloin steak, cut into thin strips	500 g
	salt and pepper to taste	
½ lb.	fresh mushrooms, sliced	250 g
1	onion, sliced	1
10 oz.	can cream of mushroom or golden mushroom soup	284 mL
1 tbsp.	Worcestershire sauce	15 mL
½ cup	skim-milk	125 mL
1 tsp.	Dijon mustard	5 mL
1 cup	sour cream OR 2% evaporated milk	250 mL

- In a large, non-stick pan, heat 1 tbsp. (15 mL) of oil over medium-high heat. To maintain the heat of the pan, cook the meat in 2 batches. Season with salt and pepper; remove to a plate and cover.

- Add a little more oil to the pan. Cook mushrooms and onions until soft, about 5 minutes. Toss and stir while cooking.

- Mix soup, Worcestershire, milk and mustard in a small bowl. Add to the pan and heat.

- Add the meat to the sauce. Stir and heat until bubbly at the edges.

- Stir in the sour cream or milk. Heat on low. Do not boil. Serve over noodles or with baked potatoes.

Serves 4

TIP: For maximum tenderness, slice the beef across the grain when cutting strips.

Golden Mushroom Sauce

A quick, rich-tasting sauce for pork medallions, meatballs or meat loaf.

10 oz.	can golden mushroom soup	284 mL
⅓ cup	beef broth OR water	75 mL
¼ cup	dry red wine	60 mL

In a small pot or microwave-safe bowl, heat and stir soup, broth and wine until smooth and heated through.

Makes 2 cups (500 mL)

Variation: For a creamy sauce, instead of broth and wine, use ½ cup (125 mL) yogurt or light sour cream and add a little chopped parsley or basil, if you have it. Heat on low, do not boil.

Zippy Meatballs

Meatballs for dinner and to store in the freezer.

2 lbs.	extra-lean ground beef	1 kg
2	eggs	2
1 cup	bread crumbs OR quick cooking oatmeal	250 mL
½ cup	skim-milk OR water	125 mL
1	small onion, grated OR 2 tsp. (10 mL) onion powder	1
1 tsp.	salt	5 mL
½ tsp.	pepper	1 mL
2 tbsp.	Worcestershire sauce	30 mL

- Preheat oven to 425°F (220°C). Spray 2 baking sheets with cooking spray or oil.

- Combine all ingredients. Shape into small balls, about 1½" (4 cm).

- Arrange meatballs on baking sheets and cook until no pink remains, 12-15 minutes. For dinner, serve with mashed potatoes and creamed corn.

- OR cool meatballs and freeze on a cookie sheet. Bag when frozen. When thawing, allow 3 per person.

- Add meatballs to pasta sauces or serve with a sweet and sour sauce, page 50, Golden Mushroom Sauce, page 128, or the Tomato Sauce below.

Serves 8

Variation: For **Turkey Meatballs**, use 2 lbs. (1 kg) of ground turkey in place of ground beef.

Tomato Sauce

Use this super-quick sauce as a topping for meat balls, meat loaf or as a 2-person serving of pasta.

2 tbsp.	chopped onion	30 mL
¼ cup	chopped celery	60 mL
1 tbsp.	water	15 mL
8 oz.	can of tomato sauce	213 mL
½ tsp.	dried basil	2 mL

- In a small bowl in the microwave, cook onion, celery and water for 3 minutes. Add tomato sauce and basil; microwave and stir until heated through, about 3 minutes.

Makes 1 cup (250 mL)

DESSERTS

Instant desserts, smoothies, fruits, sauces, crisps, cookies, cakes

Desserts make our good meals just a little more special. They can also contribute to our nutritional needs and satisfy our sweet tooth and cravings as well. Here are some quick combos from the cupboard and fridge – healthy smoothies, fruits and sauces, and new versions of everyday favorites.

Super-Quick Desserts

For a quickly prepared finish to your meal try one of these combinations or invent one of your own.

- A dish of canned applesauce topped with yogurt and a sprinkling of cinnamon sugar.

- Canned pineapple tidbits topped with vanilla yogurt or sour cream and a sprinkling of raw sugar.

- Peach slices with a few fresh raspberries.

- Stir green grapes into sour cream and add a spoonful of brown sugar. Serve immediately or refrigerate for a few hours or overnight for a refreshing, light dessert. Add a sprinkle of orange liqueur if you wish.

- Dip strawberries into sour cream and then into brown sugar. Use individual bowls for cream and sugar.

- Digestive cookies spread with cream cheese and topped with blueberry or apricot jam.

- Scottish oat cakes spread with butter and honey.

- Orange sherbet topped with crushed ginger-snaps.

- Lime sherbet topped with crushed chocolate wafers.

Ice cream and frozen yogurts always please. Here are some ideas to enhance them:

- Chocolate ice cream with raspberries and raspberry-flavored liqueur.

- Vanilla ice cream with stirred in Grand Marnier and brandy. Refreeze – very elegant – very good. Extra good with chocolate sauce.

- Coffee ice cream with crushed chocolate wafers and a little chocolate sauce or Kahlúa.

- Ice cream or frozen yogurt with a fruit salad or any of many fresh or frozen fruits. Add a little sugar if the berries or fruits are tart.

- For a **Chocolate Brownie Parfait**, crumble a brownie in the bottom of a dish, add ice cream, strawberry sauce, fresh strawberries and a little chocolate sauce. *Pictured on page 135.*

- Make a **Dessert Strata**, a sister of the trifle. Put a small slice of pound cake in the bottom of a dish. Add a layer of fruit sauce or sweetened fruit and a layer of softened ice cream. Top with more sauce and serve.

- For a **Banana Parfait**, slice half a banana into a small dish and add a scoop of vanilla ice cream. Pour Strawberry Sauce, page 133, on one side and Chocolate Sauce, page 134, on the other. Top with a few chopped, toasted pecans.

- For **Frozen Yogurt Sandwiches**, cover 12 chocolate wafer cookies with vanilla or strawberry frozen yogurt, softened a little. Top with 12 more wafers to make sandwiches. Store in a covered container in the freezer until needed.

- For an **Ice-Cream Pie**, fill a purchased chocolate or graham wafer crust with 1½ pints (750 mL) of softened chocolate or mocha ice cream. Drizzle with Chocolate Sauce, page 134, and store in the freezer, covered, until needed. Keep at room temperature for 10 minutes before cutting.

Smoothie

Mix milk, yogurt or tofu, fruit and flavorings for breakfast or for dessert.

1 cup	non-fat yogurt OR soft tofu	250 mL
1	orange, peeled and cut into pieces	1
1	banana, peeled and cut into chunks	1
2 tsp.	honey OR sugar	10 mL
1 tsp.	vanilla	5 mL

- Process all ingredients in a blender until smooth. Serve.

Serves 2

Strawberry Smoothie

Instant breakfast or lunch. The instant breakfast pouch adds a nutritional boost.

1 cup	skim-milk	250 mL
½ cup	yogurt OR soft tofu	125 mL
½ cup	sliced strawberries	125 mL
1	pouch vanilla instant breakfast (1¼ oz. [38 g])	1
4	ice cubes	4

- Place all ingredients in a blender and cover. Blend until smooth.

Serves 1

Variation: Vary the fruit content. Try banana, orange, raspberry, blueberry, peach, or a combination, fresh or frozen.

Yogurt Dip for Fruit

1 cup	plain or vanilla yogurt	250 mL
2 tbsp.	sugar	30 mL
2 tbsp.	frozen orange juice OR orange liqueur	30 mL

- Mix ingredients in a small bowl and use as a dip for fresh fruit or as a topping for stewed rhubarb or other fruit. Also, try it as a dressing for fruit salad.

Makes 1 cup (250 mL)

Cream Cheese Dip for Fruit

8 oz.	cream cheese	250 g
1 cup	sour cream	250 mL
½ cup	icing sugar	125 mL
1 tsp.	vanilla	5 mL

- Beat cream cheese with electric mixer.

- Beat in remaining ingredients. Mound in a small glass bowl.

TIP: *To prevent fruits such as apples, pears and peaches from darkening as they stand, pour 2 cups (500 mL) of lemonade over them and let stand a few minutes. Drain and arrange.*

TIP: *This recipe can be halved.*

Strawberry Sauce

Quick and delicious for cake, ice cream or pancakes.

2 cups	strawberries, fresh or frozen, loose pack, no juice	500 mL
¼ cup	orange juice	60 mL
2 tbsp.	honey OR sugar	30 mL
1 tsp.	lemon juice	5 mL
¼ cup	water	60 mL
2 tsp.	cornstarch	10 mL

- Mix strawberries, orange juice, honey or sugar and lemon juice in a small saucepan. Heat and stir until ingredients are mixed and juices bubbling.

- Combine water and cornstarch. Stir into hot sauce.

- Stir and cook until mixture has thickened and sauce is clear, about 2 minutes. Cool sauce, serve or store, covered, in the fridge.

Variation: For a **Two-Fruit Sauce**, add 1 cup (250 mL) of blueberries to the strawberries.

TIP: *recipe can be doubled.*

TIP: *For a sweeter sauce add more sugar.*

Pictured on page 135.

Chocolate Sauce

A flavorful, low-calorie, low-fat sauce for ice cream or frozen yogurt.

2 tbsp.	butter OR margarine	30 mL
2 tbsp.	cocoa	30 mL
¹/₂ cup	sugar	125 mL
2 tbsp.	corn syrup	30 mL
¹/₂ cup	evaporated skim OR 2% milk	125 mL
1 tsp.	vanilla	5 mL
pinch	cinnamon	pinch

- Melt butter in a small saucepan.

- Add cocoa, sugar and syrup. Mix. Heat over medium-high.

- Add milk a little at a time; bring to a boil and stir until smooth. Remove from heat. Stir in vanilla and cinnamon.

Makes 1 cup (250 mL)

Variation: This is a thin sauce. For a thicker sauce combine 2 tsp. (10 mL) cornstarch with the milk before you add it to the cocoa mixture. Store in a small jar in the fridge. Recipe can be doubled.

Pictured on page 135.

Maple Cream

A new taste for a whipped cream topping. Try it on the Crisp, page 140, or the Apple Pie Cake, page 141.

¹/₂ cup	whipping cream	125 mL
2 tbsp.	maple syrup	30 mL
¹/₄ tsp.	vanilla	1 mL
¹/₄ cup	chopped pecans (optional)	60 mL

Chill bowl and beaters. Beat the cream until thickened. Gradually add maple syrup and vanilla. Continue to beat until firm. Use as a topping for pies, crisps or cakes. To garnish, sprinkle with pecans.

Makes about 1 cup (250 mL), recipe may be doubled

TIP: Maple syrup can be added to non-dairy whipped toppings for a similar flavor.

DESSERTS

Fruit Salad

These fruits are available year-round. To vary, add fruits in season. This salad keeps well in the fridge for 4-5 days.

14 oz.	can unsweetened pineapple tidbits, drained	398 mL
1-2 cups	cubed cantaloupe	250-500 mL
2	kiwis, peeled and sliced	2
1	orange, peeled, sliced, quartered	1
2 tbsp.	sugar	30 mL

- Prepare fruit and mix in a glass bowl. (Add additional soft fruits such as bananas and raspberries at serving time.) Serve as is or top with ice cream or frozen yogurt.

Serves 4-6

Variation: Serve with fruited yogurt OR **Honey Yogurt Sauce**: Mix 1 cup (250 mL) yogurt, 1 tbsp. (15 mL) honey and $1/2$ tsp. (2 mL) vanilla.

Fresh Raspberries and Cream

For a beautiful presentation serve raspberries in a white dish.

4 cups	raspberries, rinsed and drained	1 L
$1/2$ cup	whipping cream, whipped just until thick	125 mL
2 tbsp.	sugar	30 mL
1 tsp.	vanilla	5 mL
$1/2$ cup	skim-milk yogurt	125 mL

- Divide rinsed berries among 4 dishes.

- Fold whipped cream, sugar and vanilla into yogurt. Spoon over berries.

Variation: For **Balsamic Strawberries**, toss 4 cups (1 L) of sliced straw-berries with a little balsamic vinegar or lemon juice, divide among 4 bowls and top with whipped cream and yogurt sauce or whipped topping.

TIP: For a sweeter version, add $1/4$ cup (60 mL) sugar to the berries.

Peaches and Raspberries

Golden peaches and red raspberries served in a pretty glass or ceramic dish make an eye-catching dessert.

4	ripe peaches	4
½ cup	lemonade OR 2 tbsp. (30 mL) lemon juice	125 mL
2 cups	fresh raspberries	500 mL
½ cup	whole almonds OR pecans	125 mL
1-2 cups	vanilla yogurt	250-500 mL

• Dip peaches in boiling water for about 30 seconds and peel. Slice. Dip slices in lemonade or lemon juice.

• Gently rinse raspberries. Drain on paper towel.

• Arrange peach slices around the edge of a plate. Pile raspberries in the middle and garnish the plate with the nuts.

• Stir yogurt and put in a serving bowl. Serve with the fruit.

Serves 4-6

Cinnamon Baked Apples

Cinnamony sweet, baked apples take less than 10 minutes in the microwave.

4	apples	4
2-4 tbsp.	brown sugar	30-45 mL
1 tsp.	cinnamon	5 mL
2 tbsp.	water	30 mL

• Wash and core apples. Leave the skin at the base intact. Remove peel in a band around ⅓ of the apple. Place the apples in a microwave dish; a glass pie plate is good.

• Half fill the apple cores with sugar and cinnamon. Pour water into the dish.

• Cover and microwave on high for 6-8 minutes, until apples are tender. Rearrange and baste halfway through the cooking time. Serve with vanilla yogurt or cream.

Serves 4

Variation: Baste apples with 3 tbsp. (45 mL) of maple syrup instead of stuffing with brown sugar.

Variation: Add a few raisins or cranberries to the cinnamon mixture.

Quick Apple Cranberry Crisp

Peeling the apples takes the most time in the preparation of this crisp. When you are in a hurry it is okay to leave some peel on the apples.

5	large apples, peeled, cored and sliced	5
1/2 cup	craisins OR fresh or dried cranberries	125 mL
2 tbsp.	sugar	30 mL
1/2 tsp.	cinnamon	2 mL
1 cup	digestive cookie crumbs, (about 9, 2 1/2" [6 cm] cookies)	250 mL
1/4 cup	chopped pecans	60 mL
2 tbsp.	butter OR margarine	30 mL

- Heat oven to 375°F (190°C).

- Put the fruit in a 8-9" (20-23 cm)micro/oven-safe pie plate or baking pan. Mix in sugar and cinnamon. Cook on high in microwave for 7 minutes, until fruit is bubbly. Stir after 3 minutes.

- Meanwhile, place cookies in a plastic bag, crush with a rolling pin. Add pecans. Transfer crumbs to a bowl and mix in butter, cutting in small pieces and then blending the mixture with your fingers. Spread crumb mixture over hot fruit.

- Place dish in the hot oven and bake until crumbs just begin to brown, about 12 minutes. Serve with ice cream, frozen yogurt or milk.

Serves 4-6

Variation: Substitute any fresh or frozen fruit; try peaches and blueberries or peaches and raspberries. Increase the microwave time for frozen fruit.

NOTE: If there seems to be an excess of juice when using frozen fruit, spoon most of it out before adding the cookie crumbs.

TIP: This recipe can be doubled and cooked in a 9 x 13" (23 x 33 cm) pan. Bake at 375°F (190°C) for 35-40 minutes, or until fruit is bubbly and the topping is golden brown.

TIP: For a sweeter taste, increase the sugar in the apples to 1/2 cup (125 mL) and add 1/4 cup (60 mL) of brown sugar to the cookie crumbs.

Peach Crisp

Speedy assembly makes this dish ready in 20 minutes.

19 oz.	can peach pie filling	540 mL
2 tsp.	lemon juice	10 mL
½ tsp.	ground nutmeg	2 mL
⅓ cup	quick cooking rolled oats	75 mL
⅓ cup	flour (whole-wheat is good too)	75 mL
⅓ cup	brown sugar	75 mL
2 tbsp.	butter OR margarine	30 mL

- Preheat oven to 375°F (190°C).

- Put the fruit in an 8-9" (20-23 cm) micro/oven-safe pie plate or baking pan. Mix in lemon juice and nutmeg .

- Cook on high in microwave for 6 minutes, until fruit is bubbly. Stir after 3 minutes.

- Meanwhile, mix oats, flour and sugar in a small bowl. Add butter to the oats. Cut in small pieces and then blend into the oat mixture with your fingers. Mixture should be crumbly.

- Spread crumb mixture over hot fruit.

- Place dish in hot oven and bake until crumbs just begin to brown, about 15 minutes. Serve with whipped topping or ice cream.

Serves 4-6

Variation: Try different pie fillings and use a little lemon juice and cinnamon or nutmeg to enhance the flavors. Try apple, cherry or blueberry.

Variation: Make **Rhubarb Crisp** in the spring. Fill the pie plate with slim rhubarb stalks cut in ½" (1.3 cm) pieces, add ½ cup (125 mL) sugar and proceed with the method above.

Apple Pie Cake

Although this takes a little more than 30 minutes to cook, it qualifies as quick cooking because it takes less than 10 minutes to prepare.

1 cup	flour	250 mL
1/3 cup	sugar	75 mL
1 tsp.	cinnamon	5 mL
1 tsp.	baking soda	5 mL
1/4 cup	pecans	60 mL
1/2 tsp.	salt	2 mL
1	egg	1
1/3 cup	vegetable oil	75 mL
2	apples, peeled and grated on large holes of grater	2
1 tsp.	cinnamon	5 mL
2 tbsp.	white sugar	30 mL

- Preheat oven to 350°F (180°C).

- In a large mixing bowl, combine flour, sugar, cinnamon, baking soda, pecans and salt. Stir well.

- Grate apples on the large holes of the food grater (apples can be thinly sliced or chopped as well. Grating is faster.)

- Stir apples into flour mixture.

- In a smaller bowl, lightly whisk egg and oil. Mix into the apple mixture. Batter will be thick.

- Spray a 10" (25 cm) pan with non-stick spray. Spoon batter into pan and spread evenly. Combine cinnamon and sugar and sprinkle over cake.

- Bake for 30 minutes, until cake tests done. Serve with whipped topping, ice cream or vanilla yogurt.

Serves 8

Variation: Use chopped fresh or frozen peaches in place of apples.

TIP: If using a glass pie pan, reduce heat by 25°F (14°C).

Oatmeal Icebox Cookies

An old-fashioned method for a favorite dessert or lunch bag cookie

1 cup	butter OR margarine, softened or at room temperature	250 mL
1 cup	brown sugar, firmly packed	250 mL
1 cup	white sugar	250 mL
2	eggs	2
2 cups	flour	500 mL
1 tsp.	baking powder	5 mL
1 tsp.	baking soda	5 mL
1 tsp.	salt	5 mL
2 cups	quick-cooking rolled oats	500 mL
1 cup	coconut	250 mL
½-1 cup	chopped nuts, pecans, walnuts or peanuts (optional)	125-250 mL

- In a large bowl, combine butter, sugars and eggs. Beat well.

- Mix flour, baking powder, baking soda and salt together and add to the butter mixture. Mix well.

- Mix in oats, coconut and nuts, if using.

- On waxed paper, shape dough into 2 rolls about 2" (5 cm) in diameter. Wrap in waxed paper or cling wrap. Dough may be stored in the fridge for a few days or the freezer for several weeks. Bake as needed.

- Heat oven to 375°F (190°C). Cut firm dough into ¼" (1 cm) slices, place on ungreased cookie sheets or parchment paper on cookie sheets, about 2" (5 cm) apart.

- Bake for 8-10 minutes, until golden and almost set. Immediately remove from cookie sheets.

Makes 4 dozen cookies

TIP: For small amounts, if you have no other reason to heat the oven, bake a few cookies in the toaster oven.

Outrageously Good Chocolate Chip Cookies

These are so good it takes a generous heart to share them. Sometimes I make chocolate chip cookies but my favorite are white chocolate with macadamia nuts. The kids like butterscotch chips with pecans.

1 cup	butter OR solid margarine, softened or at room temperature	250 mL
¾ cup	white sugar	175 mL
¾ cup	brown sugar	175 mL
2	large eggs	2
1 tsp.	vanilla	5 mL
2½ cups	sifted all-purpose flour	625 mL
1 tsp.	baking powder	5 mL
½ tsp.	salt	2 mL
1-2 cups	semisweet chocolate chips	250-500 mL
1 cup	chopped pecans OR macadamia nuts	250 mL

- Preheat oven to 375°F (190°C).

- With an electric mixer, beat butter and sugars in a large bowl until light and fluffy. Add eggs and vanilla and continue beating until creamy.

- Combine flour, baking soda and salt in a small bowl. Mix well.

- Stir flour mixture into egg mixture. Add chocolate chips and nuts.

- Drop rounded teaspoonfuls (7 mL) onto a greased cookie sheet. Bake for 8-10 minutes, until cookies are beginning to brown at the edges and set, but are still soft in the center.

Makes 4 dozen cookies

Variation: For **Butterscotch Chip Cookies** add 1-2 cups (250-500 mL) butterscotch chips and 1 cup (250 mL) chopped pecans. For **White Chocolate Macadamia Nut Cookies** add 1 cup (250 mL) white chocolate chips and 2 cups (500 mL) of macadamia nuts.

TIP: Divide the dough into 4 parts and form into rolls about 2" (5 cm) thick. Freeze or store in the fridge. To cook just a few at a time, slice off ½" (1.3 cm) pieces, place on greased cookie pan and bake. You may have to reshape the cookies a little with your fingers.

TIP: For bar cookies, spread the dough in a greased 10 x 15" (25-38 cm) pan (it will be easier to do if you use your fingers) and bake for 20 minutes, or until the edges begin to pull away from the pan and the dough in the center of the pan is just set. Cut into squares when cool.

Coconut, Chocolate Chip Bars

This is a quick, one-pan chocolate bar cookie – sweet, chewy and delicious.

2 cups	**graham cracker crumbs**	**500 mL**
¹/₂ cup	**butter OR solid margarine, melted**	**125 mL**
14 oz.	**can low-fat sweetened condensed milk**	**398 mL**
1¹/₂ cups	**chopped pecans**	**375 mL**
1 cup	**unsweetened flaked coconut**	**250 mL**
1¹/₂ cups	**semisweet chocolate chips**	**375 mL**

- Heat oven to 350°C (180°C).

- In a small bowl, combine crumbs with butter. Press evenly into a lightly oiled 9 x 13" (23 x 33 cm) baking pan.

- Pour sweetened condensed milk evenly over crumbs. Top with pecans, coconut and chocolate chips. Press down firmly.

- Bake for 20-25 minutes, until lightly browned.

- Cool and cut into bars.

Makes 24-36 bars

Chocolate Brownies

Very chocolatey, dense and delicious – and easy!

2	**eggs**	**2**
1 cup	**sugar**	**250 mL**
¹/₂ cup	**vegetable oil**	**125 mL**
1 tsp.	**vanilla**	**5 mL**
³/₄ cup	**flour**	**175 mL**
1 tsp.	**baking powder**	**5 mL**
¹/₄ cup	**cocoa**	**60 mL**
1 tsp.	**cinnamon (optional)**	**5 mL**
¹/₄ tsp.	**salt**	**1 mL**
1 cup	**semisweet chocolate chips**	**250 mL**
¹/₂ cup	**chopped pecans (optional)**	**125 mL**

Chocolate Brownies *continued*

- Preheat oven to 350°F (180°C).

- Grease a 9" (23 cm) round cake pan or an 8" (20 cm) square pan with vegetable oil or butter.

- With an electric mixer, beat eggs until fluffy; beat in sugar, oil and vanilla.

- Combine flour, baking powder, cocoa, cinnamon and salt in a small bowl or on a piece of waxed paper. Add to egg mixture. Mix until blended. Stir in chocolate chips and pecans if using.

- Spread in prepared pan and bake about 25 minutes. Brownies should be set at the edge and soft but not runny in the middle. Let cool and cut into squares.

Makes 12 slices or 25 pieces

Variation: Make a **Chocolate Glaze** and spread over the brownies before cutting. For glaze, mix until smooth: ⅔ cup(150 mL) icing sugar, 2 tbsp. (30 mL) cocoa, ¼ tsp. (1 mL) vanilla, 3-4 tbsp. (45-60 mL) hot water or coffee.

TIP: For no-mess clean up, line the pan with aluminum foil; oil the foil; bake brownies and when cool lift out of the pan.

Pictured in Chocolate Brownie Parfait on page 135.

Chocolate Butter Icing

This is a generous amount for a 3-layer cake. For a slab cake or for 2 layers cut the recipe in half and put strawberry jam between the layers.

½ cup	softened butter	125 mL
5 cups	sifted icing sugar	1.25 L
½ cup	cocoa powder	125 mL
½ cup	cream	125 mL
2 tsp.	vanilla	10 mL

- Cream butter with an electric mixer until fluffy. Gradually add icing sugar, cocoa and cream. Beat well, add only enough cream to make a thick creamy icing. Beat in vanilla.

- Spread icing between cake layers and on the top and sides of the cake.

Makes enough to frost a 3-layer cake

Chocolate Cake Supreme

Topped with chocolate icing and decorated with violets, this moist chocolatey cake is a hit every time. It's a one-bowl, no-mess favorite.

2 cups	sugar	500 mL
2 cups	flour	500 mL
¾ cup	cocoa powder	175 mL
2 tsp.	baking soda	10 mL
1 tsp.	baking powder	5 mL
½ tsp.	salt	2 mL
½ cup	vegetable oil	125 mL
3	eggs	3
1 cup	low-fat sour cream	250 mL
1 cup	strong coffee	250 mL
1 tsp.	vanilla	5 mL
1 tsp.	cinnamon	5 mL

- Preheat oven to 350°F (180°C).

- Use a 9 x 13" (23 x 33 cm) pan; grease and flour the bottom. OR use 9" (23 cm) layer pans; cut waxed or parchment paper to fit the bottoms of the pans.

- Place all the ingredients in a large bowl in order and beat at low speed with an electric mixer for 1 minute, then at medium speed for 2 minutes. Scrape bowl occasionally.

- Pour batter into pans and bake at 350°F (180°C).
  9 x 13" (23 x 33 cm): 40-45 minutes
  3 layers: 20-25 minutes – 2 layers: 30-35 minutes

- Ice with Chocolate Butter Icing, page 145. Decorate with candied or real violets for special occasions.

Makes a 9 x 13" (23 x 33 cm) slab or 2 or 3, 9" (23 cm) layers

Pictured on page 135.

Index

Share *Quick Cooking for Busy People*

Order *Quick Cooking for Busy People* at $14.95 per book plus
$4.00 (total order) for postage and handling.

Number of books_____ x $14.95 = $_____
Shipping and handling charge_____ = $ 4.00
Subtotal _____ = $_____
In Canada add 7% GST OR 15% HST where applicable _____= $_____
Total enclosed _____ = $_____

$12.95 U.S. and international orders, payable in U.S. funds. U.S. shipping $4.00.
Price is subject to change.

NAME: _____
STREET: _____
CITY: _____ PROV./STATE _____
COUNTRY _____ POSTAL CODE/ZIP _____

Please make cheque or money order payable to:
Sandy Hook Publishing
Box 202
Sandy Hook, Manitoba, Canada R0C 2W0   Telephone: 204-389-2005

For fund raising or volume purchase prices, contact
Sandy Hook Publishing. Please allow 3-4 weeks for delivery.

Share *Quick Cooking for Busy People*

Order *Quick Cooking for Busy People* at $14.95 per book plus
$4.00 (total order) for postage and handling.

Number of books_____ x $14.95 = $_____
Shipping and handling charge_____ = $ 4.00
Subtotal _____ = $_____
In Canada add 7% GST OR 15% HST where applicable _____= $_____
Total enclosed _____ = $_____

$12.95 U.S. and international orders, payable in U.S. funds. U.S. shipping $4.00.
Price is subject to change.

NAME: _____
STREET: _____
CITY: _____ PROV./STATE _____
COUNTRY _____ POSTAL CODE/ZIP _____

Please make cheque or money order payable to:
Sandy Hook Publishing
Box 202
Sandy Hook, Manitoba, Canada R0C 2W0   Telephone: 204-389-2005

For fund raising or volume purchase prices, contact
Sandy Hook Publishing. Please allow 3-4 weeks for delivery.